£12

NE

Coastal
Command
at War

Below: Z-Zebra at low height over its convoy charges. At one minute after midnight on 4 June, when some 500 miles SW of Ireland, *Zebra* received the order to 'Cease patrol' with appropriate naval thanks./*IWM*

Coastal Command at War

Chaz Bowyer

LONDON
IAN ALLAN LTD

First published 1979

ISBN 0 7110 0980 5

Design by Anthony Wirkus LSIAD

© Chaz Bowyer 1979

Published by Ian Allan Ltd, Shepperton, Surrey,
and printed in the United Kingdom by
Ian Allan Printing Ltd

By the same author:
Calshot, 1913-61
The Flying Elephants
Mosquito at War
Hurricane at War
Airmen of World War One
Sunderland at War
Hampden Special
Beaufighters at War
Path Finders at War
Albert Ball, VC
History of the RAF
Sopwith Camel –King of Combat
For Valour – The Air VCs
Guns in the Sky – The Air Gunners

Edited:
Bomber Pilot, 1916-18
Fighter Pilot on the Western Front
Wings over the Somme

**Below: Camouflaged
Catalina, AM269, BN-K of
No 240 Squadron, pictured
on 5 April 1941.**/*IWM*

'I Seek my Prey in the Sea'
(204 Squadron Motto)

'Men make the city, and not walls or ships
without men in them'
(Thucydides VIII, 7)

Contents

Introduction

The full history of RAF Coastal Command has still to be written, and it is emphasised that this volume is in no sense intended to masquerade as even a condensed history. Instead, like all previous titles in this series, this book is quite simply an attempt to re-create something of the authentic 'atmosphere' of the wartime tasks, problems, successes and – never least – sacrifices of the men of Coastal Command. It is certainly intended as one small but sincere tribute to the men of Coastal – especially the several thousands who did not live to witness the final victory over Nazidom.

Even on this lesser level, to try to illustrate the whole story of Coastal Command is clearly an impossible task within the necessary confines of a single volume. Accordingly – and I assure the reader, *most* reluctantly – I have restricted my theme strictly to the *official* parameters of RAF Coastal Command's direct control during the war period 1939-45.

The patent result of such restriction in official 'boundaries' is the exclusion of the activities of those Coastal crews who operated from bases in the Mediterranean, West Africa, and above the Indian and Pacific oceans. Equally, though strongly tempted to include much greater detail about the indefatigable and unpublicised crews of Coastal's marine craft, I feel strongly that these deserve a separate volume entirely if any sort of justice is to be done to their splendid and invaluable services.

Having apologised for the omissions, may I at least defend my selected main theme. The United Kingdom-based units of Coastal Command, later expanded to include bases in Iceland, the Azores et al, were unquestionably the prime air defence and offence – in conjunction always with Britain's traditional maritime defence, the Royal Navy – in the supremely important battle to secure shipping routes across the Atlantic ocean to and from the New World. Had the German submarine

fleet been allowed to expend its full and deadly potential for destruction, and the consequent blockade of Britain, this country could never have either survived or even pursued its long struggle with Hitler's armed ambitions. It is a plain, brutal fact that without constant replenishment by sea of vital materials, both war and domestic, this 'tight little island' would have inevitably been conquered relatively early in the war. Though virtually the least glamorous operational role, Coastal Command's unceasing efforts throughout the whole war were undeniably the base rock for Britain's ultimate survival and eventual triumph.

Many ex-Coastal men have assisted my preparation of this volume, not only by generously loaning photographs and documentary material, but also by offering their personal experiences in order to broaden my own understanding of the operational life of all Coastal crews, air and ground. Naturally the responsibility for final interpretation is mine, and any errors of fact or omission are solely mine. To each of these I offer my sincere thanks, and would particularly mention the following (in no particular order): G. Simister, DFC; W. E. Hayes; Wg Cdr D. O. Luke, RAF; A. McEwen; J. Chapman; K. R. Edney; Sqn Ldr R. H. T. Overall, RAF; F.

Haisell; R. Reeder; M. Dilks; H. Bell; R. D. Jones; S. L. Turner; K. Border; S. Lucktaylor; D. Lyall; J. H. Newland; J. Luker; P. Williams; D. M. Ryan; G. A. Stevenson; Wg Cdr W. H. Kearney, RAF (Rtd); G. E. Jones; Sqn Ldr B. H. Harvey, DFC, RAF (Rtd); Sqn Ldr S. Hare, BSc, RAF (Rtd); A. J. Watts; T. M. Jones; J. N. Rounce; E. G. Crouch; T. Kennan; R. H. Stark; J. Powell; D. Nicholson; L. Worner; L. J. Curson; W. V. Cluff; P. G. Rackliff; Wg Cdr G. C. C. Bartlett, AFC, RAF (Rtd); H. Seymour; G. Radford; J. Ford; D. A. Burns; W. S. Hurst; T. R. Wardle; E. Wilson; G. E. Haddock; D. J. Thomas; M. E. Street; ACM Sir Christopher Foxley-Norris, GCB, DSO, RAF (Rtd).

I am equally grateful for the 'normal' splendid help and cooperation offered by my good friends and colleagues, especially 'Ted' Hine of the Imperial War Museum and D. C. Bateman of the Air Historical Branch, MOD, Bruce Robertson, Ken Munson, John W. R. Taylor, Mike Bailey, Flt Lt 'Andy' Brookes, RAF, Richard Leask Ward.

Chaz Bowyer
Norwich, 1978

Below: **The Warwick ASR I version – BV301 is illustrated – built for ASR duties specifically, in which capacity it served as the equipment of some ten Coastal squadrons. In this view can be seen an airborne lifeboat slung under the bomb bay.**
/*Ministry of Aircraft Production, Crown copyright*

Heritage

Below: **On the Step. Short Singapore III of No 209 Squadron gets airborne.**
/Flight International

Above: **Felixstowe F5, N4041 taking off in January 1919. The F5 was the RAF's principal flying boat in the immediate post-1918 era, until replaced generally by the Supermarine Southampton.**
/Author's Collection

When, on 1 April 1918, the Royal Naval Air Service was forcibly amalgamated with the Royal Flying Corps to form the new Royal Air Force, the existing coastal and naval air services were abundantly healthy in men, aircraft, equipment and, not least, hard operational experience. Possessing more than 3,000 aircraft of many types, including all classes of airship, the former RNAS had controlled a long chain of coastal-located air stations stretching all along the southern and eastern coasts of Britain, apart from numerous inland training establishments and other stations. The enforced transfer to the new Service did not meet with universal approval within RNAS ranks. It might truthfully be stated that the dogmatic, unilateral attitudes of the Admiralty hierarchy since the RFC's inception in 1912 immediately found fresh grounds to continue its battles with both War Office and, especially, the newly-formed Air Council, with the constant aim of securing a monopoly of control over all aircraft, men and equipment in any manner considered to impinge on Royal Navy parameters of interest.

Recognising the delicacy of the situation, the Air Council's *Order for transferring and attaching Officers and Men to the Air Force* (sic) – promulgated in Admiralty Weekly Order 886a, dated 14 March 1918, entitled *'RNAS – Transfer to Air Force'* – made it quite plain that although all former RNAS men could and would be transferred with effect from 1 April 1918, any man not wishing to remain in the new Service could, within three months, formally be returned to the RN for completion of his individual term of service.

Nevertheless the continuing determination of the Admiralty to retain overall control of any RAF unit 'transgressing' on so-termed 'naval' areas of interest – the pursuit of which aim was to last for the following three decades in some degree – led to many compromises by the embryo Air Ministry in its almost indecent desire to try to please everybody concerned; including the 'formation' of 10 Group RAF based for administrative purposes at the former RNAS training station Calshot, Hampshire, with Wing Commander Arthur W. Bigsworth, DSO, AFC in command. ('Wing Commander' was then an RNAS rank; RAF ranks proper were not introduced until August 1919). Bigsworth's immediate superior was the Senior Naval Officer (SNO) Portsmouth. By the November 1918 armistice, Bigsworth's command included the aircraft and airship stations at Calshot, Portland, Newhaven, Bembridge, Polegate, Slindon, Upton and Cherbourg. Immediately after the cessation of hostilities Calshot was retitled as the School of Naval Co-operation and Aerial Navigation, and in 1923 became instead RAF Base, Calshot.

By December 1919 the RAF in the United Kingdom was reorganised into three Commands – Southern, Northern, and Coastal Area. The latter, which was to control all former land and air units of the RNAS, had its headquarters in Thurloe Place, London, with two Group HQs at Leuchars and Lee-on-Solent. In March 1920 RAF Coastal Area comprised just three squadrons extant, with two more in the slow process of eventual formation; while 29 Group was formed from the flights allotted to aircraft carriers still in existence – the embryo of the later Fleet Air

Above: The graceful pause as a Supermarine Southampton settles on its landing run in the Solent, off Calshot./*Author's Collection*

Left: Calshot Spit – the foremost training establishment for RAF flying boat and other maritime air crews from 1913 to the early 1950s; after which it became a maritime maintenance unit (MU) until its closure in 1961. In foreground is the centuries-old Calshot Castle, often (mistakenly) referred to as a Martello Tower; while the long hangar and adjacent slipway (left) was used by the 1929 and 1931 Schneider Trophy teams. /*Author's Collection*

Below left: Calshot Express – the tiny narrow gauge railway which conveyed many hundreds of personnel to and from the Spit at RAF Calshot during the years 1917-47. /*Author's Collection*

11

Arm. In the following month the former Southern and Northern Commands of the UK RAF became conjoined as a single RAF Inland Area.

Later in 1920 RAF Coastal Area Headquarters was transferred to the Tavistock Hotel in Tavistock Square, London, with AVM A. V. Vyvyan, CB, DSO as Air Officer Commanding (a former RN regular officer) – a building which in pre-1914 days had been something of a 'house of accommodation' for the ladies of the town to entertain their 'customers'. Night staff duty officers in those early days were to suffer a series of 'alerts' before the 'ladies' finally realised the current situation . . . Vyvyan's command was not only small but poorly equipped. All aircraft were of wartime vintage; a motley collection of flying boats, floatplanes and landplanes, with very little maintenance back-up, supplies or replacements. Overall policy was vague in intention, there being (as yet) no laid-down strategic or even tactical lines on which to base future training or equipment. Broadly speaking the heavy hand of the Admiralty was evident in most facets. Duties designated for RAF Coastal Area crews were loosely listed as protection of UK coastal waters to ensure free passage of mercantile shipping; protection of the British Fleet; assistance to the RN in mine-sweeping and spotting; *possible* offensive capability against any future enemy navy; and – least on the tabulation of priorities – anti-submarine duties.

Certainly, at hangar floor level, RAF Coastal Area was overwhelmingly naval in character and outlook in its early years. The vast majority of its air and ground crews were

men who had seen extensive naval/air service in previous years, and a uniform of 'insipid blue' (sic) hardly expunged long-term customs, even in everyday speech and slang. The result was a firmly established leaning towards a 'salty' outlook in all things, and the emergence of the 'Flying boat union' – that community of all RAF men who 'messed about in boats' (flying and sea-going), said to have originated at RNAS Felixstowe during 1914-18. Proud of their connections with both sea and air, the members of this 'union' became almost a race apart within the RAF in later years; defiantly retaining their green-buttoned (from verdigris!) uniforms and cap badges as outwardly visible signs of their calling, and slipping into pure naval jargon conversationally at virtually every given opportunity. Such fiercely guarded traditions were merely the outward manifestations of a relatively small but highly dedicated 'band of brothers'; utterly professional and exceptionally skilled men whose faith in their role was to be carried on by all future generations of Coastal crews.

The early Felixstowe and Supermarine 'boats', though adequate for in-shore coastal flying, were strictly utilitarian in design and construction. Mainly wooden-hulled at first, they had open cockpits, no heating, were cold, uncomfortable and – always – wet. Amenities for crew comfort or sustenance were non-existent. In-flight rations for any extended patrol usually consisted of sandwiches and plain water, supplemented privately by chocolate, fruit, and a flask of hot tea or coffee. Rest bunks for long flights were unknown. Even when the need for hot food and drink

Right: Mooring instruction. Ground crews at Calshot in 1932 being given the finer points of mooring a flying boat correctly. This Southampton I, the last wood-hull version, crashed on 17 October 1933, killing two of its crew.
/*Flight International*

Below: In tandem. The cockpits for two pilots and the nose gunner of a Supermarine Southampton. Note warning plate in nearest to warn pilot of proximity of the propellers behind his head.
/*Author's Collection*

became an obvious necessity in later years, these were provided for simply by installing a loose primus stove, with a locally constructed wooden box acting as the food larder. Self-sufficiency by all crews once away from base was a necessity; an affinity by most crews with their machine becoming a natural way of life, with their flying boat regarded as bed and board on many of the long-distance cruises undertaken by 'boat crews in the late 1920s and early 1930s. This affinity became manifest during World War II, particularly amongst the Short Sunderland crews.

The continuing reliance on flying boats for RAF coastal duties during the inter-war era was not wholly a matter of enthusiasm by the contemporary authorities. The financial strictures imposed by succeeding politicians forced all Service authorities to utilise existing equipment to the widest possible advantage. With a global empire to sustain, apart from territories overseas under Britain's legal mandate, the flying boat was an attractively inexpensive means of maintaining a form of air control and communication with the far-flung outposts. Requiring no aerodrome facilities, and relatively little maintenance other than that provided by the crew en route, a 'boat' was distinctly preferable to any multi-engined, large landplane in pure money terms. Nevertheless, such devotion to the flying boat by succeeding Air Ministers cannot be said to be because of any real belief in such a design's operational air/sea role; it was simply the cheapest method of offering an RAF presence abroad. Development of the flying boat in those interwar years was aimed almost exclusively at extending range and

reliability in performance; little (relatively) was put into improving its pure operational equipment for anti-shipping or anti-submarine roles.

Considering the stark fact that Britain had so very nearly been driven to the brink of surrender by the German submarine operations of 1916-17, it is relevant here to consider the almost total lack of emphasis on anti-submarine warfare by the higher authorities of those interwar years. Perhaps the chief culprit was the Admiralty in this context. After centuries of traditional experience the Royal Navy had been developed primarily as a defensive force to protect trade shipping; hence the trend had continued to build bigger and more powerful battleships for this prime purpose, backed by fast, well-armed cruisers and their attendant destroyers. Submarines were regarded as having little future as defensive weapons, and accordingly were relegated to a low priority. The idea of the submarine being a principal *offensive* naval weapon found little favour in naval circles – despite Germany's ample illustration of such a deadly role in very recent history. Such a blinkered view was even ratified with the Anglo-German Naval Agreement signed in June 1935, when the Admiralty blandly

14

agreed to a German proposal to limit German U-boat strength to about one-third (measured in displacement tonnage) of the total British Navy strength.

Unknown to the British government German U-boat development had commenced, in secret, in 1922 despite the severely restrictive terms of the Versailles Treaty on rearmament. Moreover, that development had, from the outset, concentrated on producing the U-boat as an *offensive* weapon. In September 1935 an ex World War I submarine commander, Kapitän zur See Karl Dönitz was appointed Commanding Officer for U-boats, and his primary task was to develop fighting tactics for his craft. One of the first post-1918 German commanders to believe that Germany's future enemy would be Britain, Dönitz, remembering his own experiences during the war, was sure that in the event of a war the Royal Navy would again institute merchant shipping convoys as the best method of protection for Britain's vital sea routes. Accordingly, he aimed from the beginning to introduce groups of U-boats – wolf packs – for offensive operations against such massed ship formations as a prime tactic.

Unfortunately for Dönitz, and perhaps very fortunately for Britain, his dream of a large, well-equipped U-boat force suffered to a great extent in development by the lack of enthusiasm for any naval matters by the German Führer, Adolf Hitler. Thus, in September 1939, Germany possessed a total of only 56 U-boats, of which roughly half were not capable of operating in Atlantic deep waters. Only after the early successes of these few U-boats did Hitler change his point of view, and give high priority to U-boat production. Meanwhile in Britain, the Defence Advisory Committee stated firmly that Britain would never again be blockaded by submarines as in World War I; a statement based entirely on the RN view that submarines in war would operate singly and submerged, and had therefore concentrated on appropriate defensive measures. With the start of war with Germany in 1939, the U-boats' wolf-pack tactics and their ability to attack on the sea surface took the Admiralty somewhat by surprise . . .

In 1936 the overall command structure of the RAF underwent a major reshuffle – partly in preparation for the expansion promised by various leading politicians, and also to incorporate the near-future generation of new aircraft designs beginning to come from the various British aircraft manufacturers. The first moves reorganised the RAF in Britain into four new Commands; Fighter, Bomber, Training and Coastal. Coastal Command per se came into being officially on 14 July 1936, with AM Sir Arthur M. Longmore, KCB, DSO, as its in-situ commander-in-chief, with his headquarters at Lee-on-Solent. The original Command structure (adopted in March 1936) was:

Left: **Short Singapore III, K4580 being towed ashore from the hammerhead crane at Felixstowe for compass swinging. This aircraft saw service with Nos 209, 210 and 230 Squadrons before finally being struck off charge on 14 October 1940.**
/via Grp Capt E. Shipley

Below left: **RAF 'Navy'. RAF pinnaces employed on torpedo-recovery work in the Solent c1933-34, and based at Calshot.**
/S. W. Humphries

Below: **Felixstowe scene epitomising the 'naval' character of the RAF's Coastal force, with a No 209 Squadron Blackburn Perth and attendant launch.**
/Flight International

HQ Coastal Command			
15 Group	16 Group	17 Group	FAA
6 FB sqns Marine craft Experimental Establishment	7 GR sqns 2 TB sqns	Trng stns, Lee-on-Solent Gosport Calshot Thorney Island FAA shore trng	All, except shore trng

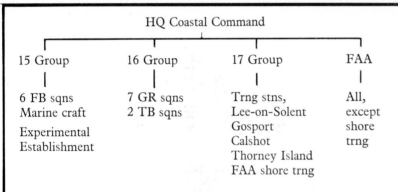

Above: **Saro Cloud K2895 leaving a Calshot slipway for a training flight in 1937. On April 6 that same year it crashed in the Solent, killing three of its passengers.**
/Flight International

However, it was found impossible to form three groups simultaneously, so the flying boat (FB) squadrons were placed temporarily under the aegis of 16 Group (formed at Lee-on-Solent in December 1936). 17 Group was also formed at Lee-on-Solent and the new administration came into being in January 1937, by then under the command of AM Philip Joubert de la Ferte. Administration and post-FTS training of the Fleet Air Arm remained under the direction of Coastal Command HQ, as did an RAF Coastal detachment in Bermuda.

Virtually the first thing Joubert instigated on taking up his appointment was an Area Combined Naval/Air Headquarters for operational control. In this central operations room RAF and RN officers sat side by side controlling their respective formations in all air/sea operations and exercises – the real beginning of a vitally necessary mutual co-operation in defence of Britain's sea life-lines. If certain members of the higher 'brass' remained strictly partisan, at least at this rather lower level mutual respect, understanding and enthusiasm found a comfortable billet, to the benefit of all. Indeed, at relatively junior

command level a degree of willing cooperation had always existed, if only on an individual basis. Differences in custom, language and attitudes had usually been matters of good-hearted humour and healthy competition between the two shades of blue uniform; so different from the entrenched and often bitter 'wars' waged along the Whitehall corridors of power. The air was a new arena, understood by relatively few very senior officers of the other two services; a novel form of warfare exclusively for the young, unencumbered by rigid attitudes or inherited prejudices.

The operational capability of Coastal Command on Joubert's appointment as AOC-in-C was reflected mainly in its equipment in the autumn of 1936. At that time the Command had a mere eight squadrons, equipped with six different types of aircraft. Four squadrons flew biplane flying boats – Nos 201 (Londons), 204 (Scapas), 209 (Singapores), and 210 (Rangoons) – while the only two units specified as torpedo bombers were Nos 22 and 42 Squadrons, each flying obsolescent Vickers Vildebeests. The remaining two units had only recently begun to re-equip with a new design, the monoplane Avro Anson general reconnaissance aircraft, first examples going to 48 Squadron, followed in June by No 206 Squadron. All other flying boat units were based overseas. Nevertheless, as with the other Commands, Coastal was on the verge of considerable expansion, and one year later its strength had risen to 14 first-line squadrons, six of which were flying Ansons, though No 228 Squadron had begun operating Stranraers, yet another biplane flying boat design. Three more squadrons came into being within the following year, while one (No 210) received the first examples of the splendid Short Sunderland flying boat. Yet, even up to the

outbreak of war, Nos 22 and 42 Squadrons continued flying the ancient Vildebeest torpedo bomber; a design at least a decade out of date for the modern requirements of such a role, thereby reflecting higher authority's lack of conviction (or interest . . .) in the torpedo as an air-strike weapon.

In fairness it should be stated that the arguments, pro and con, for the air torpedo are (were) fairly balanced in weight. Joubert himself was not entirely convinced of its efficiency – which undoubtedly influenced contemporary decisions on any urgent replacement for the Vildebeest – but he may well have been slightly biased in view of that aircraft's poor showing. Certainly, during the war, it was Joubert who pressed for the urgent introduction of a torpedo version of the Bristol Beaufighter in order to form strike wings; an aircraft with a high war performance. If little attention was paid to developing the torpedo strike role, virtually none was given to improving anti-shipping and, especially, anti-submarine weaponry. Bombs were of standard RAF design, the General Purpose (GP) type, which could have little effect on most vessels and none at all on any submerged submarine. Specific weapons for attacking marine targets simply did not exist in Coastal's bomb dumps. This may have been a side-effect of the Fleet Air Arm coming into separate being in 1937, controlled solely by the Admiralty, but was mainly the inevitable result of nearly two decades of financial neglect and parsimony for the air services by each succeeding British government during those locust years.

If the ironmongery within Coastal Command was lacking during the final years of peace, at least the future seemed brighter in respect of new aircraft designs. Chief among these was the four-engined, monoplane Short Sunderland flying boat – a metal-clad behemoth which offered greater range, endurance and, incidentally, crew comfort on long patrols. Further replacement designs for the existing biplane 'boats included the Saro Lerwick and the Blackburn TBR Botha – both in the event to prove costly failures – while on 15 October 1938 the new Bristol Beaufort first flew in prototype form. Already aware of the overall deficiency in sheer numbers of aircraft for first-line operations, a British Purchasing Commission visited the USA in April 1938, resulting in an initial order for 200 military versions of a twin-engined Lockheed 14 airliner, later to enter Coastal Command service as the Hudson in early 1939 with No 224 Squadron at Leuchars.

On 18 August 1937 Philip Joubert was succeeded as AOC-in-C Coastal Command by AM Sir Frederick W. Bowhill. A man with unrivalled maritime experience – he had originally entered RN service in 1898 as a midshipman – 'Ginger' Bowhill had seen wide and varied experience in the RNAS and the RAF. Shortly after taking up his appointment, Bowhill moved the command headquarters from Lee-on-Solent to a private house, Eastbury Park, at Northwood, near Watford, taking with him what became the pattern of the future Command Operations Room. This latter was built inside an inconspicuous wooden building, part-protected by natural earthwork and camouflaged from aerial view by surrounding trees. From this inauspicious building Bowhill was to direct the fortunes of Coastal Command for the next four years. Inside this control centre was the simplest possible lay-out; comprising one wall entirely covered by a map on which all movements by aircraft, ships et al could be

traced. Facing this map were three small rooms, one each for the Army, Navy and RAF controllers and their small staff, though in the event the 'Army Room' was taken over by the embryo Air/Sea Rescue operations' controller, Wg Cdr H. J. Tanburn. Based little more than 20 miles from the Admiralty and Air Ministry in London, the 'Ops Room' was thus in close contact with the chiefs of both services throughout the coming war.

The imminent prospect of war with Germany had been realised early in 1939 – one might truthfully say since the September 1938 Munich 'Crisis' – and Coastal Command units first received their mobilisation orders on 24 July 1939, in order to bring them into the following position by 14 August 1939:

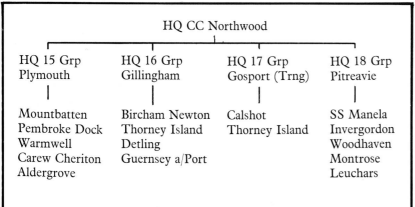

HQ CC Northwood			
HQ 15 Grp Plymouth	HQ 16 Grp Gillingham	HQ 17 Grp Gosport (Trng)	HQ 18 Grp Pitreavie
Mountbatten	Bircham Newton	Calshot	SS Manela
Pembroke Dock	Thorney Island	Thorney Island	Invergordon
Warmwell	Detling		Woodhaven
Carew Cheriton	Guernsey a/Port		Montrose
Aldergrove			Leuchars

The various Group functions were already defined for war, these being flexible as operational circumstances decreed, but in general were:
Anti-submarine patrols   15, 18
Anti-shipping   16, 18
Operational training on CC aircraft   17
Met flights & ASR   All groups
PRU   106

Actual aircraft strength of the Command on 3 September 1939 was:

Avro Anson   301
Lockheed Hudson   53
Vickers Vildebeest   30
Short Sunderland   27
Saro London   17
Supermarine Stranraer   9

In addition were several one-off individual communications aircraft – a gross total of nearly 450 aircraft; of which perhaps half were truly first-line in availability on that date. The actual figure for personnel serving within the aegis of Coastal Command that day is unknown precisely, but did not exceed 10,000 men and women of all ranks or status.

The immense task facing Coastal Command throughout the World War II conflict commenced on 2 September – a day prior to the actual declaration of war – and was to continue *every* day, and night, until well after the official cessation of hostilities in 1945. That task was possibly (some would say, definitely …) the prime task allotted to the RAF during the whole war – the protection of the sea highways surrounding Britain, and the country's lifelines for virtually every commodity across the Atlantic Ocean. For a nation with centuries of proud maritime tradition in its past, Britain had always seemed to have produced seamen of a calibre guaranteed to preserve her sovereignty from the jealous ambitions of her rivals. The men of RAF Coastal Command on that fateful day in September 1939 were the latest examples of such a proud lineage – 'seamen' of the air who, with those who joined them in later years, upheld their splendid heritage.

Left: Officer Training Corps cadets board a Saro London of No 201 Squadron at Calshot on 3 August 1939. /*C. Peckham*

Below: Enter the Annie. Avro Ansons K6207 (M), K6206 (L) and K6204 (N) of No 220 Squadron in 1937. The nearest Anson, M, eventually went to Canada in February 1941 for further service./*Author's Collection*

Bottom: The Queen. Short Sunderland L5806 in its pre-1939 silver livery. It later saw service with No 10 Squadron RAAF, and Nos 228 and 230 Squadrons. /*Short Brothers*

Kipper Patrol

Below: Convoy. A scene epitomising the bulk of Coastal Command's prime responsibilities throughout the years 1939-45./*IWM*

Top right: Royal visit. HM King George VI, accompanied by Air Marshal Sir Frederick Bowhill and Kingsley Wood, Secretary of State for Air, during a tour of Coastal Command HQ at Northwood /*Author's Collection*

Bottom right: Toothless Tiger. The ubiquitous De Havilland 82, Tiger Moth trainer, which was impressed briefly for anti-submarine 'scarecrow' patrols during the war's early months. /*Author's Collection*

On the outbreak of war in September 1939 Coastal Command was faced with a multitude of problems and responsibilities. As with virtually every other Command in the RAF, the chief problem was simply quantity of suitable aircraft with which to undertake its myriad of tasks and duties. Coastal's prime role at that time was air protection of the United Kingdom's in-shore waters and the shipping lanes to and from Britain along which must flow the bulk of Allied and domestic vital supplies and material. The German submarine was the obvious main threat to Britain's sea life-lines – surface raiders, though of near-equal potential threat, were thought to be capable of being mastered by Britain's Royal Navy, aided by the relatively small Fleet Air Arm.

Faced with such an enormous task, with comparatively few operational aircraft with which to accomplish it, Coastal Command was forced to improvise. On the simple precept that no submarine could attack shipping if fully submerged below periscope depth, the idea was mooted that 'scarecrow' patrols would, at least, prevent a fair proportion of potential sinkings. As long as some form of air cover was constantly available over the approaches to most main inlets and harbours, no submarine commander was likely to risk his ship and crew by remaining at shallow periscope fighting depth. Necessarily the concept was of the 'prevention is better than cure' theory, but Coastal Command in the early months of the war had little or no alternative. Thus, in December 1939, six Coastal Patrol

Flights were brought into being, located at strategic points around Britain's coastline. These were situated:

No 1 CPF   Dyce (Aberdeen)
No 2 CPF   Abbotsinch (Glasgow)
No 3 CPF   Hooton Park (Birkenhead)
No 4 CPF   Aldergrove (Belfast)
No 5 CPF   Carew Cheriton (Tenby)
No 6 CPF   St Eval (Newquay)

Each CPF was established for nine aircraft, with at least six pilots, but the aircraft allocated were all De Havilland Tiger Moths, except No 6 CPF, which flew DH Hornet Moths; open-cockpit, fabric and wood-structured biplanes, bereft of radio, armament, or any other warlike impedimenta, and barely capable of achieving a normal cruising speed of 75kts. Sole armament was a signal pistol, while communication could only be gained by use of two homing pigeons, carried in a wicker basket in the spare cockpit. Personal flying clothing for the solitary pilot was comprised of normal Sidcot suit, fur-lined jacket, or any other type of privately supplied clothing available; and the only concession to personal preservation in the event of a ditching in the sea was a part-inflated motor car inner tube, with a 30ft length of string attached to a marine distress signal . . .

The first 'scarecrow' patrol by No 1 CPF was flown on 14 December 1939 along the east coast of Scotland, but three days later a Tiger Moth pilot spotted a periscope and started to dive towards it. The periscope quickly disappeared into the depths, but the 'scarecrow' had at least achieved its purpose. Tiger patrols were normally flown by pairs; thus, if any U-boat was sighted, one Tiger Moth could return to base and summon armed help, while the other kept tabs on the U-boat. If within visual range of any RN ships the Tiger pilot could at least fire a green Very Light signal cartridge, then circle the U-boat's location.

Throughout the winter of 1939-40 – the bitterest cold winter in living memory – the Tiger crews plodded around Britain's coasts, enduring severe icing, fiendishly cold temperatures, and grinding monotony of hours of fruitless search. At least two 'scarecrow' pilots are on record as actually falling asleep in mid-patrol. One only awoke as his Tiger Moth's wheels dipped into the sea; while the second returned to base and was startled to find a bunch of sea-weed trailing from his tail skid – he had absolutely no conscious recollection of ever being near the sea surface . . . ! If the months of apparently pointless 'scarecrow' patrols bore minimal known results, they justified their existence admirably on 25 January 1940. On that date Flg Off P. C. Hoyle of No 1 CPF, in Tiger Moth N6841 took off at 2.20pm from Dyce, in company with Pilot Officer Child (N6845). Nearly an hour later Hoyle spotted an oil slick which was apparently moving steadily, and signalled by Very Light to some nearby destroyers:
'To help the destroyer I repeatedly dived at the head of the oil line, the last dive, in my excitement, being a race for it past the bows of the destroyer. Climbing sharply I turned in time to watch the ship pass its whole length

Above: **Supermarine Stranraer BN-L of No 240 Squadron, still soldiering on as late as 22 April 1941.** */Author's Collectiion*

Left: **The scene in Lerwick harbour on 22 November 1939 after a German bombing raid. Saro Londons of No 201 Squadron moored out, with L7042 burning furiously in the foreground.** */No 201 Squadron, RAF*

Centre left: **Armstrong Whitworth Whitley GR VII of No 612 Squadron getting airborne from Reykjavik, Iceland, 1942 (despite the optical illusion to the contrary . . . !). The normal festoons of radar ASV 'stickleback' aerials along its spine have been eliminated here by a wartime censor.** */IWM*

Bottom left: **Whitley GR VII, YG-R of No 502 Squadron, based at St Eval in 1942, on anti-submarine patrol. Though something of a hasty improvisation, the GR Whitley units were responsible for sinking or seriously damaging at least 15 U-boats.** */IWM*

23

Below: Ordered in large quantity by the RAF prior to the outbreak of war, the Lockheed Hudson saw wide service with Coastal Command during 1939-45, apart from other Commands. Here a Mk I, T9277, of No 233 Squadron displays the contemporary camouflage scheme of doping./*IWM*

in front of the oil, and then let fly about six depth charges in a pattern. These exploded with fearful crashes a few seconds later. The sea was illuminated deep down and appeared to jerk upwards, causing a spray on the surface. This subsided, only to be followed by giant upheavals. Apart from the usual black sort of scum caused by depth charges, more oil came up and the line ceased to go forward.'

Though no U-boat was actually claimed as destroyed on this occasion, oil continued to seep up for several weeks thereafter, and another destroyer later dropped yet another pattern of depth charges on the spot. It was virtually the only highlight in the history of the 'scarecrow' patrols – by June 1940 the CPFs were quietly disbanded and their pilots dispersed to other duties. They had achieved no directly tangible results, but no one would deny the potential value of the Tiger Moth 'Jim Crow' sorties, nor can the pilots' courage be degraded.

It would not be overstating the case to say that the real backbone of Coastal Command during the early years of its existence was the Avro Anson – 'Faithful Annie' as it was universally dubbed by its crews. Indeed, the RAF in general owed a heavy debt of gratitude to the Anson, which served in a bewildering variety of roles from 1936 to 1967, during which period some 11,000 Ansons were built. The prototype, K4771, first flew on 24 March 1935, and Service testing was carried out at Gosport by the Coastal Defence Development Unit there. Ordered in quantity for the RAF, the Anson was the Service's first twin-engined monoplane having a retractable undercarriage. In its original military guise the Anson was powered by twin-cowled Cheetah VI engines, later changed to Cheetah IXs of 350hp each, giving the Anson a range of at least 600 miles at a cruising speed of (perhaps . . .) 160mph. For armament the design incorporated a gun turret amidships, containing a single, hand-operated Lewis machine gun, and a fixed, forward-firing Vickers gun for the pilot. Bomb load of up to 360lb weight could also be carried.

Specified initially as a Coastal reconnaissance type, the Anson first entered RAF service in 48 Squadron, Coastal Command on 6 March 1936 at Manston. Tasked with training air crews for maritime reconnaissance duties, 48 Squadron soon became the largest Anson unit in sheer numbers. Other Coastal units were quickly formed with the type, including Nos 217, 220, 206, 224, 233 and 269 Squadrons; and by the outbreak of war 11 squadrons within the command were flying Ansons. These included four Auxiliary Air Force (AAF) units – Nos 500, 502, 608 and 612 Squadrons – which became part of Coastal Command 1938-39. Employed on coastal patrols, convoy protection, and anti-submarine sorties from the outset of hostilities, Ansons were among the first aircraft to attack U-boats. On 5 September 1939 a No 206 Squadron Anson (K6187/E) dropped two 100lb bombs on a U-boat without visible result; while on 3 December another No 206 Squadron aircraft (K6184/P) released its bombs onto the conning tower of another surfaced U-boat. Its pilot, Plt Off R. H. Harper, was awarded a DFC for his determination in this attack.

Though classified as obsolescent for first-line operations by 1940, Ansons continued to fill the gap for many Coastal units until late 1941. Apart from normal over-sea patrols, Ansons were on occasion used to bomb enemy-held ports and harbours, and during the initial stages of the BEF's evacuation from Dunkirk, were active in preventing German surface vessels from interfering with the cross-Channel evacuation shipping. Lamentably slow and lumbering when compared with contemporary aircraft, the Anson was nevertheless a fighter in every sense of the word when the occasion demanded pure air-to-air combat. Prominent in the active role were the 'Annies' of No 500 Squadron, AAF based at Detling. During May 1940 alone the unit's Ansons accumulated a total of 1386 operational flying hours; but the squadron's highlight came on 1 June.

A patrol of three Ansons, led by Plt Off Philip Peters in 'V', were sent off to do a daylight patrol between Dunkirk and Ostend. Keeping to a mere 50ft height above the sea, the trio were jumped by a gaggle of nine Messerschmitt Bf109s just after 10.40am. All three Ansons were armed with additional side guns, installed as a result of squadron initiative. As the first Bf109s bore in from the rear the Ansons split formation, and Peters was left to bear the brunt of the attacks. By throttling back at propitious moments, and utilising the Annie's well-known ability to skid-turn sharply, Peters managed to foil

Left: **Hudson cockpit, pictured on 5 May 1942.** */IWM*

Below left: **A No 206 Squadron crew about to start a patrol in Hudson T9303, 'V'.** */Flight International*

Below: **Hudson on its bombing run (approaching camera) over a German convoy on 6 May 1942, with bomb doors agape.** */IWM*

several onslaughts; while his gunners eventually shot two Bf109s into the sea and sent a third scurrying off seriously damaged. The whole affair lasted less than 10min, but the Anson emerged triumphant and returned to base unscathed. Peters was awarded a DFC, while DFM awards were given to his erstwhile crew, Sgt Deryck Spencer, Cpl L. G. Smith and LAC L. S. Dilnutt.

Peters' outstanding combat was, however, merely one of many engagements with the Luftwaffe by No 500 Squadron's lumbering Ansons. On 24 June the rear gunner of Anson 'N', Sgt Prentice, destroyed a Bf109; on 18 July Sgt Barr saw four Bf110 two-seaters harassing the convoy he was protecting and promptly 'waded in'; fighting all four Zerstörer for several minutes and finally sending one Bf110 into the sea in flames. In September Plt Off Armstrong Brown tackled a pair of Henschel 126s, driving both off, and was then beset by three Bf109s. Sending one of these down probably destroyed, despite receiving wounds, Brown then regained his base safely and later received a particularly well-deserved DFC. By the close of the daylight Battle of Britain No 500 Squadron's

Above left: Early casualty.
Q-Queenie of No 233
Squadron displays its flak
scars on return from
Norway, 1940./*IWM*

Left: Flt Lt W. H. Biddell of
No 206 (Hudson) Squadron,
who was awarded a DFC in
1940 for air fighting, and
who was the pilot of a
Hudson in which General
Sikorski and his staff were
evacuated safely from
Bordeaux to England, to
form a new Polish army and
air force./*IWM*

Above: Open-air servicing
on Hudson I, N7303 of No 269
Squadron. In background is
Anson K6244, also on No
269's charge, 1940./*IWM*

Right: Hudson I, S-Sugar of
No 48 Squadron. The light
yellow square patches on
wing and tailplane were gas
detection panels – a 1940
idiosyncracy./*IWM*

tally of enemy aircraft amounted to six confirmed as destroyed, with a further five probably destroyed or at least seriously damaged; an indication of the Anson's toughness and its crews' fighting spirit. Part-exemplifying that aggressive attitude was the fitting of a cannon, firing rearwards, on one No 500 Squadron Anson. It was said that the recoil added an extra five knots to the speed . . . !

By the close of 1941 most Ansons had been replaced in firstline Coastal squadrons by Hudsons, Blenheims or other more advanced aircraft designs; though a number were modified to accept ASV gear and other submarine detection 'black boxes' and soldiered on until late 1942. Some of the intended replacement aircraft were by no means as successful as the faithful Anson, however. One example was the twin-engined, shoulder-wing Blackburn Botha. Designed as a land-based reconnaissance/bomber, and having internal stowage for a torpedo, the Botha first entered Coastal service with No 608 Squadron AAF in June 1940, and flew coastal sorties until 6 November. Thereafter the Botha was relegated to training duties, which it performed well until late 1944.

Another 'new' design from which much was expected was the twin-engined Saro Lerwick flying boat. Reasonably heavily armed – having three power-operated gun turrets in the nose, tail and dorsal locations – and a useful top speed in excess of 200mph, with a normal range of 1,500 miles; the Lerwick was ill-starred. Service trials reported poor take-off and general flying performance figures, but the urgent necessity of Coastal Command's commitments during the early war years forced the Lerwick's introduction to operations. Entering service with No 240 Squadron at Calshot in June-September 1940, the first all-Lerwick unit was No 209 Squadron when No 240's aircraft were transferred to replace No 209's last Supermarine Stranraers in early 1941. The Lerwick's subsequent war record was a fine blend of accidents, failures, and few worthwhile successes. Only one other Coastal unit received Lerwicks; No 422 Squadron RCAF, which flew the type from July to November 1942, though not operationally. Too heavy, aerodynamically unstable, with low engine reliability, the Saro Lerwick saw relatively little action, and achieved even less.

Below: **The ill-starred Saro Lerwick; in this view, L7265 which served briefly with No 209 Squadron as WQ-Q in early 1941, but was struck off RAF charge at the close of 1941 with less than 200 flying hours in its log.**/*IWM*

Valiant and Brave*

On 15 November 1939 a new, bulky-looking twin-engined monoplane torpedo-bomber was delivered to Thorney Island for intensive flying trials by No 22 Squadron. Having been equipped with the obsolete Vickers Vildebeest biplane for over five years, the crews of 22 Squadron warmly welcomed this updating in weaponry, the all-metal Bristol Beaufort proving to have more than twice the speed of the Vildebeest, with double the biplane's striking range. Moving to North Coates on 8 April 1940, No 22 Squadron was joined there by its sister torpedo unit, No 42 Squadron; the

*Preux et Audacieux - official motto of No 22 Squadron, RAF.

latter already in the process of exchanging its out-dated Vildebeests for Beauforts. For the following five months both squadrons were employed on mining and bombing sorties only, incurring a crop of casualties almost equally due to recalcitrant Beaufort engines as enemy action; but on 11 September five Beauforts of No 22 Squadron, led by Flight Lieutenant Dick Beaumann, set out on the unit's first true torpedo operation to attack an enemy convoy off Calais.

By the close of the year No 22 Squadron's crews had flown 36 torpedo sorties in the English Channel area, making low-level attacks from close range on a wide variety of

Below: **Bristol Beaufort, with training torpedo tucked under its belly.**/*Central Press*

31

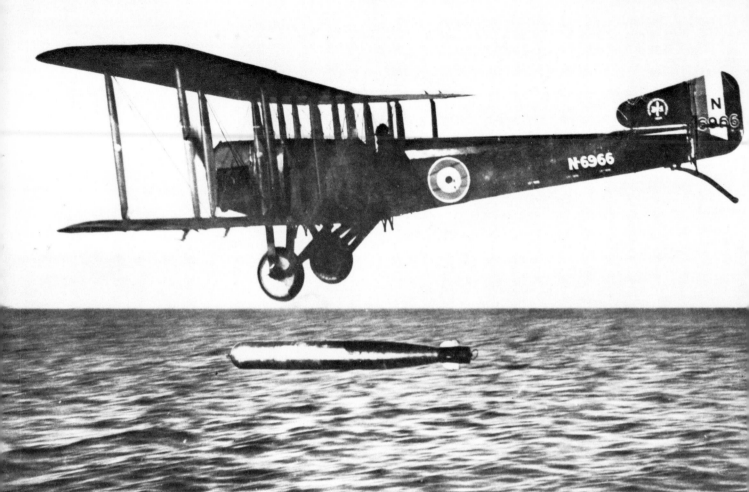

Top: In the beginning . . .
Sopwith T1 Cuckoo, N6966,
demonstrates a perfect
torpedo drop in 1919.
/*Author's Collection*

Above: Vildebeest IVs of
No 42 Squadron, based at
Thorney Island, on a practice
torpedo attack just prior to
the war. The nearest
aircraft, K8080, was sent to
the RNZAF in 1940.
/*Author's Collection*

enemy shipping in what were known as Rover operations. In October 1940 three new pilots to the squadron were posted in; Jimmy Hyde, an Australian in the RAF, Pat Gibbs, and a Scotsman from Saltcoats, Ayrshire, Ken Campbell. Hyde was to have a distinguished career in torpedo bombers for the next two years, before being killed in action while leading 86 Squadron's Beauforts from Malta. Ken Campbell was destined to earn undying fame for his ultimate torpedo sortie on 6 April 1941 when he attacked the German battleship *Gneisenau* in Brest harbour and was killed in the attempt. His supreme valour that day brought him the posthumous award of a Victoria Cross. Third of this trio was Pat Gibbs, an ex-Cranwell cadet who had just completed a year at the Air Torpedo Training Unit at Gosport as an instructor and, with promotion to Sqn Ldr, joined No 22 Squadron as its latest C Flight commander. Gibbs, though not a brilliant pilot, was dedicated to his task – one might even say obsessional about it. An idealist and perfectionist in most things, Gibbs was eventually to rise to Wg Cdr, DSO, DFC, and become overall commander of the torpedo strike squadrons based on Malta, attacking Rommel's vital supply shipping lines feeding and replenishing the German Afrika Korps. Finally, in 1944, Gibbs was invalided out of the Service, having extended both his physical and nervous systems to the extremes in pursuing his dedication to torpedo work.

One of his earliest operational sorties with No 22 Squadron took place on 30 November 1940 – a mixture of success and near-tragedy, which exemplifies the hazards and circumstances surrounding most early torpedo strikes:

'At noon, a sighting report came from Dick (Beaumann) of a convoy in a position off Texel steaming east. He had attacked, the report said, but without result. My navigator quickly worked out a course to intercept the convoy, based on its speed and position given in Dick's report, and after a few minutes discussion on the attack we should make, John and I were off to our aircraft; the sooner we could get to the convoy, the less time it would have to disperse or go into harbour.

'This was not a Rover operation, but a definite "strike", and so bad weather could only be hoped for and not demanded as our "right". But as we neared the enemy coast cloud seemed scarce; there was just an occasional white cloud high out of reach in a clear blue sky, with no sign of a cloud-bank anywhere. However, I pinned my faith in my navigator bringing us straight on to the convoy without having to spend a dangerous time searching. I then intended to make a quick attack and run unashamedly for home before fighters could answer a call from the convoy and come out to intercept us.

'The navigation proved accurate, for before even the outline of the coast was visible a forest of masts and a haze of smoke could be seen projecting above the horizon dead in front of us. As we approached low over the water they became smoking funnels, and finally the stately hulls of ships steaming in convoy. Visibility was unlimited, making the coastline beyond the convoy appear ominously near, and the time taken to reach the target infinite, for we must have sighted it first from something approaching 20 miles away. I felt naked in a sky owned and swept clear by the enemy. This was a strange insidious "land", bathed in lethal blue sky and unwanted sunshine. As we drew nearer I could count eight ships in the convoy, steaming in line-ahead and flanked by flak ships positioned as a screen just at torpedo range from the ships they were protecting. As mile succeeded mile I was confidently expecting that they would sight us and open fire; yet, strangely, nothing happened. All was peaceful and silent as a summer's day, which in fact that last day of November perversely resembled with its hot sun shining through the perspex in my cockpit and the sea matching the sky in their two colours of blue.

'During the long approach I had been manoeuvring to reach a position ahead of the convoy, intending to turn there and fly towards it rather than approach it from the side where I would be seen from every ship. At last I could no longer see the ships as long majestic hulls rising and falling gently in the swell which prevailed, but as narrow, top-heavy shapes rolling regularly from side to side – than I turned towards them. It was my intention to fly along parallel to their course, prepared to turn in to the attack as soon as I came abreast of the largest ship, or when the flak started, whichever happened first. Thus we passed within a mile of the leading ship, flying so low along its length that we might have been flying fish temporarily out of our element yet these tactics were effective for we passed unseen. By this time the open sky above me had inured me to danger, for we had been flying under it for some minutes within sight of the enemy and there was still no sign of fighters. I felt that the flak from the ships, which must start at any minute, was a small danger compared with an attack by fighters. Flak was encountered often and its dangers overcome as an everyday occurrence, but fighters were unknown and dreaded.

'We passed the second ship in the convoy, all the time nearing the fourth and largest ship on which I had my eye, and still we appeared to be undetected. My feeling was one of suspicion and pleasant disbelief; it was too good to be true. The acute tension which

had been present when the target was first sighted had been killed dead by the long flight to the horizon, and was now replaced by an apathetic curiosity. During the whole approach we were the thieves of time, for all the while we should have been under heavy fire, with fighters on their way to intercept us; instead we were running down the line of enemy ships under a clear sky, picking and choosing the biggest target. The situation was unreal, the open sky, the steadily steaming ships with the beaches and green fields of Texel behind them, and John and I, within a mile, about to attack.

'The mile separating us from our target would become less by painful hundreds of yards, until torpedo range was reached. Seconds would split into agonising tenths as with the attack the game would start in earnest, we would declare our presence, the torpedo would enter the water with a splash, a glove dropped to challenge the defences, and as we turned away our engines would roar at full throttle as we avoided the fire from a hundred guns. I rocked my Beaufort's wings just slightly, hardly daring to attract attention, an upraised eyebrow of a signal, but sufficient to send John out of formation and ready to attack. Then I turned in towards the 10,000-ton ship which was my target, steaming slowly and serenely northward unaware of its danger. I ran in towards it, finger on the torpedo release button and an occasional glance

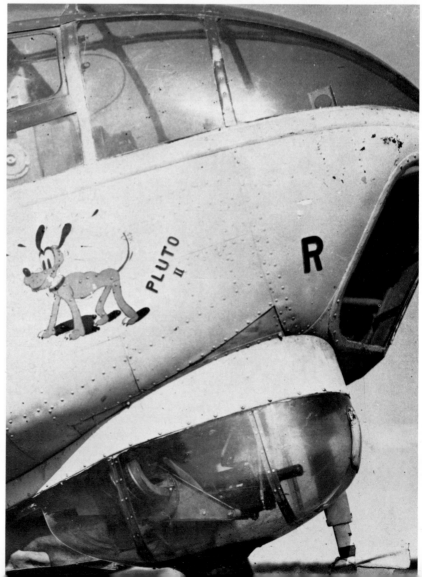

34

at the airpseed indicator to check our speed, but my eyes rarely left the ship which steamed across my sights, or the flak ship which we had to pass to reach the dropping position.

'Where was the flak? I almost prayed for flak to start to relieve the unbearable tension. I was just within dropping range and taking a steady aim, when a single stream of tracer crossed in front of me, silver rain against a blue sky, but port-flare to gunpowder. I had dropped my torpedo and was turning away when the convoy became no longer an inoffensive line of ships but a solid fortress. The flak came as never before. It is only the "usual", I said to myself, no worse, no thicker, no more accurate, no more deadly than before; just the "usual" tracer and daubs of black smoke hanging absurdly in the air around my Beaufort, just the crackling of flames and tongues of fire from a wall of guns. Light shells can do no harm, I told myself, and remembered those three impotent shells which had hit my aircraft, it seemed years ago. Taking violent avoiding action, I never let the Beaufort settle down on a steady course for a split second, always turning first one way and then another, alternatively climbing and diving to outwit the defences and seeing streams of tracer flying wide first on one side and then on another. I thanked Providence that I had taken the precaution of flying not

in my usual flying suit but in my shirtsleeves, for this violent flying caused sweat to stream off my forehead; perhaps fear had a little to do with it also! In another moment, a pregnant one, we had reached the safety of extreme range, when the fire was comparatively innocuous and could be ignored, and I had time to relax after the ordeal.

'For me the critical time of the whole day had arrived. During the time when I had been jinking to avoid the AA fire my torpedo should have been running steadily towards the target; was this to be another miss or my first success? I was turning almost reluctantly to see the result of the attack, when my gunner shouted briefly and triumphantly, "She's up!"; a statement I could hardly wait to prove with my own eyes. Turning quickly, I was just in time to see a column of water falling back like an extinguished fountain around the stern of the ship I had just attacked. The heavy black smoke of explosion still enshrouded the afterpart of the vessel long after the cauldron of foam had died away. As the smoke cloud in its turn rose to hang like a canopy over the doomed ship, she began to sink slowly by the stern, her bows rising gently from the water. In her last moments she was still stately and unhurried, a torpedoed ship sinking beneath the waves. My aim had only just met its mark. The extreme stern had been hit, when only a few feet could have

Top left: A No 22 Squadron Beaufort crew climbing aboard, and demonstrating various forms of entry to the aircraft./*Central Press*

Bottom left: Beaufort R-Robert's personal Disney cartoon character insigne '*Pluto II*'; painted just above the chin gun emplacement of a single, remotely-fired .303in Browning machine gun for undertail protection. /*PNA Ltd*

Above: Pair of No 42 Squadron Beauforts out on patrol. Nearest aircraft is L9965, with a 'private' name *Mercury* painted on side of the nose compartment./*IWM*

separated me from yet another miss. I tried to imagine as I looked at the ship now heeling over drunkenly and giving up her last breath quite how I should have felt if the torpedo had slid harmlessly past the stern and I blessed those few feet which had made the difference between success and failure.

'Fascinated, I wanted to stay and watch the final plunge, but John's (Flg Off J. Barry) Beaufort, once more in formation and hugging mine, reminded me of the open sky and the inevitable call for help which the convoy must have made. It could only be a few minutes before an avenging swarm of fighters would be on the scene. We left with the ship's final sinking unwitnessed; two Beauforts flying close together as one aircraft, hugging the surface of the water, leaving destruction in their wake. I had not been able to keep an eye on John during the attack, and for all I knew he might have aimed his torpedo at the same ship, but my observer told me he had seen him attacking a ship right at the end of the convoy without any result. However, one big ship for two torpedoes seemed enough for one day, and John himself indicated how pleased he was at our success by grinning broadly and gesticulating as he flew alongside me.

'We reached the aerodrome just after three o'clock in the afternoon, to find the Winco and

Centre left: **Wg Cdr R. P. M. 'Pat' Gibbs, DSO, DFC, of Nos 22 and 39 Squadrons and Malta fame. An ex-Cranwell cadet, Gibbs became one of the RAF's leading exponents of the airborne torpedo.**/*IWM*

Left: **Flt Lt R. 'Dick' Beauman, DFC, of No 22 Squadron, who was killed in action flying Beaufot L9936, 'B' during an attack on Wilhelmshaven on 5 December 1940.** /*via R. Barker*

Below: **She's up! An air-launched torpedo finds its mark.**/*via R. Barker*

all the other crews lined up on the tarmac waiting for our story, for our signal had already been received giving bare details of our attack. Excitedly we scrambled out of K-for Kitty almost before she had come to rest, and gabbled our versions of what had happened to the audience which surrounded us. Meanwhile John landed and his crew came up to join us in the story with picturesque details which had escaped us, of sailors jumping into the sea as our torpedo approached and boats being lowered as the ship settled down. Was the convoy worth another strike? asked Winco when all had been said, and were the other ships torpedo targets? Certainly there were four or five other ships of between five and eight thousand tons which were well worth attacking, we said, but could they be reached before sunset?

'There followed frantic activity. Our aircraft were refuelled and loaded with torpedoes while I rushed to Operations Room to report very briefly on what had happened. Group rang up asking to speak to the pilot who had been out on the "strike" and, picking up the receiver, I heard the voice of the AOC himself asking "Is the cloud cover sufficient?" In reply I abandoned caution under the bright light of success and did my best to lie convincingly, "Yes, sir, it's quite adequate for a quick attack". And so we were sent off once more.'

Gibbs and another Beaufort flew back to the convoy but on reaching the area could find nothing to attack – solid darkness had by then obscured any possible sight of a target. Frustrated, tired from the aftermath of excitement and then depression at finding no targets, the pair of Beauforts, reluctantly turned for home base.

'Good navigation and "George's" accurate flying brought us to a point on the Lincolnshire coast south of the aerodrome, as we had intended, for there were balloons to be avoided northwards and we always made a southern landfall in case of error. I took over from "George" (automatic pilot) and followed the coast northwards, flying by instruments and directed by my navigator, for it was a pitch-black night in which I could see nothing. It was with pleasant surprise that I suddenly saw the aerodrome far ahead, a bright flare-path shining distinctly in the night. I made a quick circle of the aerodrome, flashing my letter, K,K,K for Kitty, to which the answer was a green light from the flare-path – permission to land.

'With undercarriage lowered, flaps down, and airscrews in fine pitch, I approached the

Right: Grp Cpt (later AVM) Francis Braithwaite who commanded No 42 Squadron in 1940. He was killed in a Meteor jet aircraft crash in December 1956./*IWM*

Below: Beaus abroad – Beauforts of No 86 Squadron setting out en masse on 15 October 1942./*IWM*

aerodrome, not very steadily, not quite aligned with the flare-path, onto which I attempted to turn. Slowly I drew nearer to the first flare, losing height each second, feeling confident of a safe landing and anticipating the sudden glare of the floodlight and then the firm feel of the ground beneath my aircraft's wheels. I had been in the air eight hours that day, and was unknowingly very tired. Fatigue spelt carelessness, and this now hurled my Beaufort from the sky to the ground. I was straight in my approach now, confident of a steady landing, when I made the careless mistake; I took my hand from the twin throttles controlling each engine to make an adjustment to the cockpit light. The throttle levers, momentarily unsupported and loose, closed as if moved by an invisible hand, causing both engines to die away. I saw the flare-path, by which I was guided, suddenly reel drunkenly ahead as I appeared to dive beneath it; my hand went instantly to the throttles, the engines roared to life again, but too late.

'The aircraft struck the ground with a sickly concussion of metal, only to rebound into the air again, turning slowly over and

Above: **Attack – Beauforts raiding St Peter Port, Guernsey in the Channel Islands.**/*MOD (Air)*

Right: **The No 42 Squadron crew who crippled a battleship. Flt Sgt Ray Loveitt (2nd from 1) and his crew Downing, Morris and Wallace-Pannell, who in the Beaufort behind them, titled 'W-Wreck', torpedoed the German battleship** *Lutzow* **on 13 June 1941; putting the vessel in dock for at least six months. Loveitt was awarded a DFM, and later commissioned.** /*via R. Barker*

Above: Kiwis. Hampdens of
No 489 Squadron, RNZAF,
which served with Coastal
Command as a torpedo and
general attack unit. Nearest
Hampden is AE361,
'C-Charlie'./*IWM*

40

over until it struck the ground with a final blinding crash of disintegration. My last conscious memory was of the flare-path appearing to be moving across the sky above me, but this curious sight brought no realisation that we were turning over in the air; I was past such speed of thought and firmly in the grip of the calamity I had caused. Everything had happened so quickly; when I should have been completing an uneventful run-up the flare-path my Beaufort lay a wreck in a field adjoining the aerodrome, and I and my crew lay stunned and injured among the wreckage that had flown out that day as Beaufort K.

'Between the field and the aerodrome was a typical Lincolnshire dyke, which prevented the ambulance reaching us immediately, since it had to make a lengthy detour. It was Jimmy who pulled me out of the twisted metal and shattered glass in which I was lying half stunned. He had waded, fully clothed, through the intervening dyke, and now worked hurriedly to get us out and away from the aircraft, for petrol was everywhere and fire might break out at any minute. By this time I was quite conscious and found myself covered in blood from some head wounds, and also large quantities of Lincolnshire earth into which I had been thrown by the crash. Jimmy afterwards told me that I never ceased to curse fluently as he helped me out of the wreckage, and that I then walked about supporting my right arm (broken) with my left hand. All I remember is that my right arm was quite useless and that I was little help to Jimmy in extricating the rest of the crew. However, my wireless operator was quite uninjured, merely a little dazed, and we found him wandering round the field trying to work out what had happened to him. Together the three of us managed to lift the navigator and gunner out of the wreckage and lay them on the ground. Petrol, blood and earth, all surrounded by twisted metal, were illuminated by the light of Jimmy's torch. Blackness of night was all around and the noise of other aircraft could be heard circling the aerodrome; the flare-path which I had failed to reach was still alight and mocking me as the ambulance at last came to carry away our useless bodies, not to fly again for many months.'

Below: **Hampden crews of No 144 Squadron at Leuchars, prior to the unit's detachment to Russia (Vaenga) in September-October 1942, in company with No 455 Squadron RAAF.**/*W. D. Barrett*

Sub~Kill

Although more than a million flying hours were expended by Coastal crews on operations throughout the war, seeking – primarily – to locate and destroy U-boats, the number of submarines actually sighted, attacked and destroyed was, statistically, relatively small. If, however, the number of U-boats destroyed by aircraft is set against the total of U-boats actually employed by Germany, the figure becomes more realistic – roughly one in five, or approximately 20 per cent. Add to that figure almost as many more U-boats damaged, crippled, and forced to abandon their sorties and return to a safe harbour for necessary repairs, and the tally rises to almost one in three. Yet even to sight a U-boat was rare – understandably so when it is realised on just how vast a canvas the Atlantic battle was painted. Those relatively few crews who did have the good fortune both to sight and destroy a U-boat pressed home their attack instantly and with the utmost determination – a prey so elusive had to be killed instantly if at all. The difference between an aircraft sighting any U-boat and reaching it to attack was seldom more than one minute. A fully surfaced submarine could submerge in any emergency in at least 30-40sec. The void between life and death for a U-boat crew was thus less than 20sec in a majority of cases.

The men who served in submarines – be they German, British, or any other nationality – were always volunteers, just as the air crews of the RAF were. It needed a particular form of courage to serve in submarines in war. A description of the submariner's conditions at sea was once given by an RAF officer, Wg Cdr J. Romanes:

'The greatest hardship is a lack of space in which to live and breathe. Most craft are some 200ft long, with a maximum internal diameter of 15ft, and the hull shape is almost round. Throughout almost the entire length

Left: **Confirmed kill. U-625 in its death throes after attack by Sunderland EK591, '2-U' of No 422 Squadron, RCAF, on 10 March 1944. The flying boat skipper, WO2 W. F. Morton was on his first sortie as captain, screened by Flt Lt S. W. Butler.** */Public Archives of Canada*

of the boat half of this space is taken up by the huge batteries, six main ballast tanks, two quick-diving tanks and many for trimming, fresh water, fuel etc. About a third of the remaining space is occupied by engines and main motors and a quarter of the rest by torpedo tubes and allied gear. These leave a very small space to be divided into control room, officers' and crews' quarters, galley, petty officers' quarters and lavatory. Space overhead is further restricted by miles of pipes to all ballast tanks, high and low pressure air, associated valves, hydraulic and hand-operated, battery cabling, and a mass of other gear.

'The control room has to house wireless, Asdic, echo-sounder, steering and hydroplane steering gear, as well as a 10-man watch. Living quarters are necessarily minute. The Wardroom (four officers) is some eight by six feet; while 20 men live in the foc'sle, 20ft long by 7ft wide for'ard and 10ft wide aft. Hammocks fill all available space, and to get through them usually meant crawling. The lively behaviour of the boat in a seaway makes movement difficult; she literally whips about. Moreover, the deck is so greasy with diesel oil that even in a slight sea it's an art to stay on one's feet.

'Normally the submarine dives all day, which can mean 16 hours – six in the morning to ten at night. [This was written before the introduction of the Schnorkel tube in German U-boats.—*Author*.] During this time the forty-man crew uses up its limited supply of oxygen in the air trapped in the boat. The effects of oxygen starvation are soon felt. It becomes more of an effort to move around, reading is difficult – effects very similar to flying at great height without oxygen. To avoid fouling the air more than absolutely necessary neither smoking or cooking is permitted. Lavatories must be used as little as possible as these are operated by pressure air and when blown releases a bubble of air to the surface. Smells are impossible to prevent, with crew, engines, diesel oil and batteries all making a contribution; so that when the hatch is opened on surfacing, fresh air tastes foul and one gets a heavy coat of fur on one's mouth which makes the first cigarette taste

43

disgusting. Moreover, when the boat is submerged a powder is put down to absorb some of the carbon monoxide in the boat, which mostly succeeds in making the crew cough violently. Moisture condenses inside the hull of the boat and after a few days there is a perpetual drip everywhere which saturates all blankets on bunks and, of course, personal clothing.'

Romanes' description does not include the added terrors of operating under such internal conditions. If submerged the crew could always hear Asdic 'pings' and the splash of depth charges – any depth charge dropped within 40-50 miles could often be heard inside every submarine within such an underwater range. To endure depth charge attacks for (occasionally) up to 24 hours – a total of perhaps 2/300 DCs – needed supreme nerves, especially when it is realised that no one could know where (or when) the next DC might detonate. Inside any U-boat under DC attack chaos reigned – lights would extinguish, gauges shatter their glass covers, crockery shatter, loose objects fly around. And should sea water gain access to the batteries and mix with the sulphuric acid, the result would be chlorine gas, highly poisonous and a choking

Right: **Flt Lt William Roxburgh, DFC, a Glaswegian, who piloted Fortress FK195, 'L' of No 206 Squadron on 25 March 1943 from Benbecula, and sank U-489 with depth charges during his patrol.**/*IWM*

Below: **Boeing Fortress II, FL459, 'J' of No 206 Squadron taxying at Benbecula, Azores, late 1943. Also flown by crews of Nos 220, 519 and 251 Squadrons later, FL459 was eventually scrapped in December 1945. Note underwing and nose ASV radar antennae.**/*IWM*

death. It is seldom appreciated in the present climate of nuclear-powered submarines capable of girdling the globe, fully submerged that a World War II submarine when surfaced could achieve little more speed than a man on a bicycle; while under water the maximum speed for evasion of attack or retreat was little more than a man's walking pace. The main salvation was a deep, fast dive – *if* time permitted . . .

The following individual accounts of positive U-boat kills are but representative of all such confirmed victories. With few exceptions those aircraft captains who eventually achieved at least one U-boat kill were men who had spent anything up to 1,000 flying hours over the sea, hunting, searching, seeking their prey, without sight of a single enemy submarine until that moment. Yet, in every case, their reaction was immediate – attack.

Flt Lt Bill Roxburgh, a Glaswegian, was skipper of Fortress FK195, 'L' of No 206 Squadron on 25 March 1943, flying yet another monotonous 'water-watching' patrol when his 'moment' came.

'We'd been stooging around for hours when, as we emerged from a cloud, someone shouted over the intercom, "Look-out". He was so excited he couldn't say another word. Less than two miles away was a U-boat, a peach of a target. I was too high and too close to make an orthodox attack, and I knew if I circled down he'd crash-dive before I could get there, so, as seconds counted, I thought I

Above: Consolidated PB4Y-I Liberator of No 110 Squadron USN, based at Dunkeswell and Upottery variously from October 1943 to April 1945. One of six squadrons of Fleet Air Wing Seven, formed in mid-1943 to relieve 479th BG, USAAF of all its anti-submarine commitments. Cooperating with 19 Group HQ, the FAW7 provided almost half of its daily operational aircraft for direct control by Coastal Command. No 110 Squadron alone flew 1,741 sorties from October 1943 to April 1945; making 16 direct attacks on U-boats. /*Author's Collection*

Left: Near-miss. Depth charge explosion during Catalina 'K' of No 202 Squadron's attack on a submarine on 9 February 1943. The U-boat escaped without serious damage on this occasion. /*Author's Collection*

Above: The track of a
Sunderland's rear guns
straddle U-518 on 27 June
1943. The aircraft, 'P' of
No 201 Squadron, piloted by
Flg Off Laine, succeeded in
seriously damaging the
U-boat, which abandoned
its patrol.
/No 201 Squadron, RAF

Right: Sound and fury.
U-106 in the midst of a
combined attack by two
Sunderlands on 2 August
1943; the aircraft were 'M'
of No 461 Squadron,
skippered by Flt Lt Irwin
'Chick' Clarke, RAAF, and
JM708/'N' of No 228
Squadron, Flt Lt R. D.
Hanbury. The submarine
exploded shortly after this
photo was taken, and sank
vertically./*BIPPA*

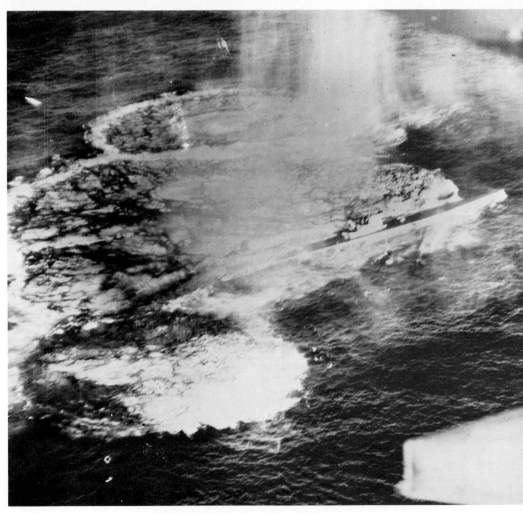

might as well crack right in. I pushed everything forward and down we went, touching 270mph!

'Everyone in the aircraft became momentarily unstuck, but our drill stood us in good stead and as the crew picked themselves up from the floor they scrambled to their action stations. The front gunner, who had been standing beside me, reached his turret and cordite fumes blew in my face when he opened at point-blank range and pumped fire into the side of the sub. We could see his bullets slapping off the metal. Away went the depth charges and, as I pulled out of the dive with all my strength and then banked around, I saw our target submerging with a pronounced list to port and making very little way.

'A little while later it popped up again, bows first, at a very steep angle and with a rolling motion. By then I'd got into position for the more usual pattern of attack and when it made its second appearance I flew in again – but it disappeared, rather shakily this time, before we got over it. However, we dropped our DCs on the spot and results were soon apparent. There was a terrific underwater explosion and bits of wood, cylindrical objects, a huge piece of wood that looked like

the top of a long table, a bundle that looked like clothes, all "jack-in-the-boxed" to the surface.'

Roxburgh's victim had been U-489, which disappeared with all hands. Just over six weeks later Wg Cdr W. E. Oulton, commander of No 58 Squadron, destroyed U-663; then on 15 May 1943 made a second kill. 'We had a lengthy patrol in Halifax "M" and were feeling pretty brassed off. We had dived down several times to investigate suspicious-looking objects on the sea, all of which turned out to be small trawlers. Then we saw yet another wake. "Another trawler", we thought, as I pushed the control column forward, "but we'd better have a look anyway". I had my lunch on my knees at the time and was munching bread and butter and tomatoes. At four miles' range I suddenly realised it was no trawler but a U-boat. I tensed and sat up straight without a thought to my lunch; the plate flew off my knees and spilled all over the cockpit floor.

'As we ran in to starboard I saw the U-boat ploughing through rough seas, which were occasionally breaking over the conning tower. There seemed to be no one on the deck or conning tower – I think no one could have

Below: Additional 'muscle' for Coastal Command was the Lockheed Ventura GR2 in late 1943, after the type's withdrawal from bombing duties. Capable of lifting a 2,500lb bomb load, and up to eight 3in rockets on under-wing launching rails, the Ventura had sufficient operational range to be truly effective in the maritime struggle./*Author's Collection*

stood that rolling without being pitched overboard. Probably the crew were keeping dry below deck and maintaining only a periscope watch. When we passed over the sub just for'ard of the conning tower, the bomb aimer let go the depth charges. For a few seconds I thought we'd overshot and felt like swearing hard. Then the rear gunner's voice came over the intercomm, "Right against her port side, sir. Good show." I started to turn, with the gunner burbling comments into the microphone, "Her bow's lifting . . . the whole fore-part is out of the water . . . she's going down!"

'A few seconds later I saw it for myself. It was an astonishing sight. Straight up in the air stuck the bows of the U-boat, some 50ft of them. It looked just like Cleopatra's Needle. Then, as though a giant hand was slowly pushing it down, the bow – still vertical – started to sink in the water. Soon only 20ft of it were left, and in about three minutes it had disappeared. We saw no survivors at all and I believe Jerry must have been caught flat-footed. The depth charges must have torn his hull open at the stern before he even knew he was being attacked, and the rush of water into the rear compartments pulled the stern straight down. They must have all died

like rats in a trap.' [Oulton's target was U-463.]

Flt Lt W. B. Tilley, RAAF, a skipper of No 10 Squadron, RAAF, flying Sunderlands from Mount Batten, sank his first U-boat on 8 July 1944. Flying Sunderland 'H', Tilley was on patrol across the notorious Bay of Biscay that day, and had reached a spot some 130 miles south-west of Brest when his second pilot, Roy Felan, said, 'What do you make of that over there?' Tilley, taking a spell in Felan's seat, looked, then jumped right up and took over the captain's seat:

'I sounded the U-boat warning and the crew jumped to action stations. I'd done 550 hours of operational flying since I arrived in England, but this was the first U-boat I'd ever seen and I was a bit excited. We turned in immediately to attack but before I finished the turn the U-boat must have seen us because it opened fire. The flak was pretty thick. We went straight for them, using fairly violent evasive action until we were 2,000yd away. We expected to be hit at any minute so I opened up with my four fixed nose guns. I could see by the splashes in the sea that our fire was falling short, so I ceased and then opened up again when we were 1,500yd off. This time I could see the spray coming up a little to port of the U-boat. It wasn't difficult then to keep the fire on the conning tower.

'We stopped evasive action while I concentrated on the guns and as the flak was coming

Top left: **Grp Capt W. E. Oulton, DSO, DFC, when commanding RAF Azores. As a Halifax skipper with No 58 Squadron, Oulton sank U-463 on 15 May 1943; then shared in the destruction of U-563 on 31 May. He eventually retired from the RAF as Air Vice-Marshal CB, CBE, DSO, DFC.**/*IWM*

Bottom left: **Last plunge: The stern of U-463, sunk by Wg Cdr W. E. Oulton in Halifax M/58 on 15 May 1943.** /*Author's Collection*

Right and below: **Flg Off W. B. Tilley, RAAF, and with his crew at Pembroke Dock. Tilley was skipper of Sunderland 'H' of No 10 Squadron RAAF on 8 July 1944, when his attacks sank U-243.**/*IWM*

up pretty thick, I kept saying to myself, "We're going to cop it". Just before my guns ceased firing there was an explosion in our bow compartment, but this was later found to be a cartridge exploded in the breech of one of our own guns. The U-boat made no attempt to submerge and I kept thinking, "When are we going to get to the bloody thing". The gunfire seemed to stop at 400yd and we could see the sub, nice and grey and sleek, on the water. The Germans ceased fire at 400yd and our guns at 300yd. We were flying then at 140kts at 75ft above the sea. Then I dropped the DCs. Crew drill was perfect and the only break in the silence over the intercomm was the navigator, Flight Lieutenant Ivor Wood, giving calm running commentary, and his instructions to the wireless operator regarding signals to be sent (to base).

'After we had passed over we evaded in case they re-manned their guns. Then pandemonium broke out over the intercomm. The tail gunner had given the U-boat a final burst as we ran over, and he saw the results of our drop ."You beaut, you've got him!" We then circled at a quarter of a mile to watch results of our handiwork. The U-boat was low by the stern but one gun kept popping at us. The second pilot had been out of it up to then and asked me what he could do, so I told him to get the hand-held camera. He then took photographs all the time out of one of the hatches, as the U-boat slowly sank.

49

Above: Flg Off K. O. Moore, RCAF, of No 224 Squadron who, on 8 June 1944, made Coastal history by sinking two U-boats within 22 minutes – U-629 and U-413, in Liberator G-George. Moore was awarded an immediate DSO for this feat of arms./*IWM*

'Then a United States Liberator from No 105 Squadron arrived and made two runs over the U-boat, firing at it but dropping no depth charges. We kept circling. Then one of our squadron's Sunderlands came along, with a fellow Australian, Dick Cargeeg, as captain. He dropped depth charges but the U-boat had ceased to move. White smoke was coming from the conning tower and some of the Germans climbed out. Cargeeg's DCs fell 30yd ahead and slightly on the port bow – he'd allowed for the U-boat still making way – but he got some good photographs showing the Germans lined up on the deck, with about 15 yellow dinghies. They were abandoning ship.

'The US Liberator made another attack and dropped eight depth charges near the sinking U-boat. The blokes were in the water at this time and must have been fairly shaken up by the DCs. The U-boat was now sinking fast and went down tail first, almost vertically. The survivors were in the water and I made a run over them with a camera. There were two big dinghies and 15 one-man dinghies. One of the men I could see had a red and black striped pullover on. The dinghies looked very yellow in the water. I kept running over out of curiosity and they were waving to us and we were waving back. I felt a bit sorry for them so I dropped one of our dinghies and two food packs.

'By this time the Liberator and the other Sunderland had stooged off, but we stayed over the sinking U-boat as long as we could and then flew back to base with only ten

minutes petrol to spare. At eight o'clock that night the Germans were picked up by a Canadian destroyer, the *Restigouche*. We had killed 14 of them with our guns, and 37 of them came back to England alive. The Germans talked to the destroyer crew and said that the captain of the U-boat [It was U-243. *Author*] exposed himself on the conning tower as we were firing, and his head had been chopped off. It just fell on the deck.'

Though several Coastal skippers finished the war with one or more U-boat sinkings credited, only one captain ever accounted for two U-boats sunk within a single patrol. Flg Off K. O. Moore, RCAF of No 224 Squadron. 'Kayo' Moore's crew of his Leigh Light Liberator were a typically mixed batch of nationalities; seven Canadians, an Englishman, Scotsman and a Welshman. On every operational sortie they carried a crew mascot, 'Warrant Officer Dinty', a stuffed panda bear, rigged out in mini-WO's uniform and sporting an observer's half-wing brevet. Already 'awarded' the original 1939-42 medal, 'Dinty' was later officially notified by letter from RCAF HQ of his award of a DFM . . . On the night of 7/8 June 1944, Dinty – wearing proudly his brand-new DFM ribbon – was aboard Liberator 'G-George' when Moore set out for an anti-submarine sweep; part of Operation Cork designed to seal off the western end of the English Channel from any U-boat attempting to attack the Allied invasion fleet off Normandy. By the time Moore had begun his designated 'beat' the

Above centre: The official badge of No 224 Squadron RAF. Formed originally in Italy in 1918, the original badge painting was 'countersigned' by the Italian dictator Benito Mussolini in 1938 – and the motto, in Italian, translates as 'Faithful to a friend'. . . ! /*Author's Collection*

Above and left: Leigh Light. The brilliant (in every sense) invention of Sqn Ldr Humphrey de Verde Leigh, an administration officer at Coastal HQ in 1940, which later proved to be of enormous help in submarine detection by night./*IWM*

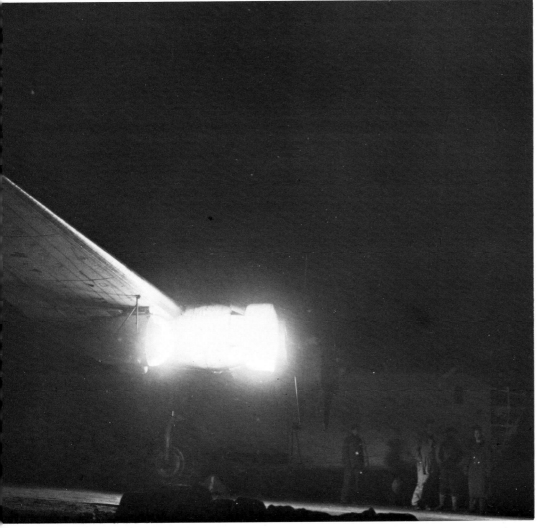

Above: **Killer cat. The Consolidated Catalina (JX637 here) with which at least nine RAF squadrons were equipped, apart from RCAF and USN units. 'Cats' sank or seriously damaged at least 45 U-boats; while two Cat skippers were awarded VCs. Though not of outstanding general performance, the Cat's extreme range of some 4,000 miles made the type an essential facet of the Atlantic air 'bridge' cover for Allied shipping.**
/Boeing Aircraft Company

first of a total of 42 U-boats were beginning to penetrate the Cork patrols' zone, and in the early hours of 8 June Moore's radar operator reported a contact, some 12 miles ahead. The night was bright moonlight, with near-perfect visibility, so Moore decided not to use his Leigh Light. As he approached the contact spot, he saw a U-boat, fully surfaced:
'It was a perfect silhouette, as if it were painted on white paper, and I could make out the conning tower perfectly. As we approached at 40ft height we could see the U-boat's crew had been taken by surprise. About eight German sailors on deck, apparently in utter confusion, were running like hell to man their guns. The U-boat commander [Oberleutnant Bugs, U-629. *Author*], however, made no attempt to crash-dive, and those manning the guns waited for us to close the range. Al Gibb, our front gunner, opened fire when we were within 1,000yd and scored repeated hits on the conning tower and deck. Simultaneously the Germans opened fire on us. I took evasive action while Gibb continued to blaze away, and then tracked over the conning tower. The flak had been silenced during the last yards, and as we released our depth charges in a perfect straddle I saw one of the crew in the "bandstand" double up and fall overboard into the water.

'The U-boat seemed to jump into the air and explode, splitting wide open. I made a steep turn. On the water we could see wreckage and large patches of oil. As we stooged around for another five minutes we saw black objects in the water, probably bodies.'

Highly elated with their success, Moore's crew continued their patrol 'beat', having still six depth charges and a homing torpedo in the bomb bay. Moore's report continues: 'As we resumed patrol over the Channel Mike Werbiski was busy at the wireless set sending out a flash report to advise Coastal Command HQ that we had just made an attack. Almost immediately WO MacDowell, the Scottish navigator, who at the time was adjusting the bomb sight, shouted a warning that he could see another U-boat ahead, travelling fairly slowly. It was a small U-boat and remained fully surfaced, making no attempt to avoid a fight. As we closed to attack Al Gibb opened up from the front turret, and we met heavy flak, which came up in the shape of a coloured fan. Going straight through all this we roared over the conning tower and dropped the remaining DCs, getting a perfect straddle according to my rear gunner. After this run the U-boat was still on the surface but listing heavily to starboard.

Left and below: Cat's teeth. The side blister guns of a Catalina; initially twin VGO .303s, then .50in Brownings respectively./*IWM*

'As we circled I saw the bow of the U-boat rise 25ft out of the water at a 75deg angle, then slide back into the sea. We made a third circuit over the spot where the U-boat had vanished. Three dinghies were in the water with three or four sailors in each, then we resumed our patrol.'

Moore's second victim that night – sunk only 22 minutes after the first – was U-413, whose commander Oberleutnant von Lehsten and 43 of his crew survived and were later retrieved from the sea. Moore was awarded an immediate DSO for his unique achievement, while three other crew members received the DFC or DFM. 'Warrant Officer Dinty, DFM' was unofficially awarded a Bar to his DFM . . .

Far left: Short Sunderland EK591, U-Uncle of No 422 Squadron, RCAF, on the point of landing at Castle Archdale, Northern Ireland, on 15 July 1944. It was this Sunderland which sank U-625 on 10 March 1944. /*Public Archives of Canada*

Left: Aerial depth charges – simply adapted variants of the naval Mk VII DC of World War I vintage-design – seen here on the mobile under-wing bomb racks of a Sunderland. By 1943 modified DCs, capable of positive explosion at a mere 25ft shallow depth, entered Coastal service, with greatly improved results over the early models. /*Author's Collection*

Below: Camouflaged Catalina, AM269, BN-K of No 240 Squadron, pictured on 5 April 1941./*IWM*

Ops in a Wimpy

Throughout the years 1939-45 Coastal Command operated a wide variety of aircraft types in its constant pursuance of combatting each new threat or tactic in the Atlantic battle. Judged solely by the number of U-boats actually sunk or at least severely damaged by the close of the war, the Liberator proved to be the most successful; accounting for nearly one-third of all successful claims. Closest in such an achievement came the doughty Sunderland, but – perhaps somewhat surprisingly to the layman – the Sunderlands' final tally was almost equalled by an aircraft never intended for maritime operations – the Vickers Wellington bomber. By May 1945 Coastal Command Wimpys accounted for 51 U-boats sunk or so seriously damaged that they were forced to abandon their patrol and return to harbour.

The Wellington first entered the Coastal scene at the very start of the war. Alarmed by the menace to shipping of the magnetic sea mines being sown by the Luftwaffe around Allied ports and sea lanes, a hasty counter-measure was devised, tested, and put into operational service – all within three months; the DWI Wellington. A 51ft diameter ring, containing an aluminium electro-magnetic coil, was constructed at Vickers' Weybridge works in November 1939, and then fitted underneath Wellington Ia, P2516, and first air-tested at Boscombe Down on 21 December. Known as the Directional Wireless Installation (DWI), its magnetic field could, within limitations, be 'focused' to detonate sea mines by flying low and steadily over any reported or suspected mined zone. By Spring 1940 the DWI Wimpy had been proven successful, if ungainly, and a small number were issued to Coastal units, while one example was sent to North Africa where other Wellingtons were suitably converted with components sent out separately. Sweeping the Mediterranean coastal area and, especially,

Below: **Stickleback. Blackpool-built Wellington Mk XIII, JA144, fitted with spinal ASV radar aerials, and having carriage for torpedoes.**/*IWM*

the vital Suez Canal linkway, was undertaken by DWIs of No 162 Squadron among other units. Soon after its introduction, however, the DWI Wellington was superseded by the de-gaussing apparatus fitted to merchant shipping.

With the gradual introduction of radar further RAF Coastal Command uses for the sturdy Wellington soon came into being. Suitably modified Wellingtons were tested as pure torpedo bombers, with a modicum of success in trials, but the first true Coastal Wimpy version put into broad operational service was the Mk VIII. Virtually a modified Mk Ic, the Mk VIII was produced in both day and night variants; the day type having ASV Mk II radar, with appropriate 'Stickleback' antennae along its back and underwing 'Yagi' aerial, for detection and then torpedo roles. The night variant was fitted with a retractable Leigh Light aft of the bomb bay and depth charges. Later Wellington Marks added refinements to the Mk VIII version, in the light of operational experience, resulting in many hundreds of Wimpy torpedo or Leigh Light variants seeing first-line service with the maritime squadrons. By the end of the war nearly 2,400 Wellingtons, of all marks, had been built solely or experimentally for maritime roles.

Of all the types of Wellington used by Coastal Command, the most successful – in terms of U-boats sighted, attacked, sunk and/or damaged – were those used on Leigh Light sorties. The first-ever Leigh Light operational use took place on the night of 3/4 June 1942, when Squadron Leader Jeaff Greswell of No 172 Squadron was on patrol in a Wellington over the south-west area of the Bay of Biscay and detected the Italian submarine *Luigi Torelli* on the surface. On his second attack run, Greswell released a near-perfect straddle of depth charges across the submarine, causing severe damage but not sinking her. The first Leigh Light 'kill' came on 6 July 1942 when another pilot of No 172 Squadron, Plt Off W. Howell (an American) sank U-502. Gordon Jones, who served as a wireless operator/air gunner ASV with No 36 Squadron from May 1944 to the end of the European war, mainly operated the ASV Mk III radar set in the Wellington XIVs of the squadron. His personal account of his year with No 36 Squadron is modest: '. . . nothing very spectacular happened, it very seldom did on GR squadrons, but the fact that we were there, sitting over the U-boats even when we didn't know it, must have stopped a few of their little games – at least, we used to be told this.'

Gordon Jones first joined No 36 Squadron, with the rest of his crew – comprising captain, second pilot, navigator and three W/Os – in May 1944 at Reghaia, some miles from Algiers, North Africa. Over the following months No 36 Squadron flew a variety of sorties in different roles – anti-submarine over the Mediterranean, bombing, reconnaissance, dropping 'Window' during the Oper-

Below: **The DWI (Directional Wireless Installation) fitted here on a Wellington 1c conversion, HX682 of No 162 Squadron, on 6 August 1943; the unit being based in the Suez Canal area at that date. DWI was rendered unnecessary in UK coastal waters when suitable degaussing rings were available for ships, but continued in use overseas for several years.**/*IWM*

ation Dragoon preliminaries to invading southern France – and by September was based at Tarquinia, Italy. Taking up the account at this point in time, Gordon Jones continued:

'We only did one or two ops from Tarquinia as the squadron was given a whole week off flying. The CO, being a good type, decided to send one flight at a time to Rome for a couple of days. I think B Flight won the toss and went first. Within two hours of their going we were called together and told that No 36 Squadron was posted to the UK, and had to get off the following day! Half the squadron was by this time in Rome and well spread out. The remainder of us had to get all the aeroplanes ready, everything packed, and do all the other necessary things. I've never seen such a panic – no one wanted to be left behind! We hung kit bags in the bomb bays and stuffed the aircraft with all the odds and ends. Meantime messages for No 36 Squadron people were posted in all the canteens and NAAFIs (and other places . . .) in Rome. Our boys saw them, naturally, but since they were not told why they had to return to base, quite a few chose to ignore the order – after all, who was to know if they had seen it or not? They did all return the next day, I believe.

'We worked hard and got, if I remember correctly, about 18 out of 20 Wellingtons ready to go for next day. Needless to say the weather closed in and we did not go in fact until the day after. The trip back to UK was uneventful, over cloud most of the way, and we landed at St Mawgan where they had meals ready for about 150 bods. The rest of the squadron went on to Chivenor for some reason or other, not having received the message to land at St Mawgan. Our crew had a lonely meal – I often wonder what happened to all that food which had been prepared. We changed money and went through the Customs, which was rather difficult as all the kit was still in kit bags in the bomb bay, tied up with bits of string and wire. As I recall the Customs officer decided to trust us. We then took off for Chivenor, it was dusk and we found everyone on the station lined up watching us land. Apparently some wag had started a rumour that we were a new crew that had never done a night landing before . . . they were disappointed.

'We were given a fair amount of practice flying to get us used to operating from the UK with all its nav aids etc, and we became operational on 3 November, when we did an anti-U-boat patrol in the Channel in NB884, RW-H; a night trip of 9½ hours. Most of our ops were to be patrols of this kind; mostly at night and lasting 10 or 11 hours. The longest trip I did was 11hr 50min – which in those days seemed a long time in a noisy old Wimp.

During the working up period quite a few incidents occurred, including my own first night flight from Chivenor. Having landed quite safely after a practice trip, we then spent about 1½ hours taxying around in the mist trying to find our correct dispersal. We would taxi for a few hundred yards and then have to stop while the brake pressure built up again to have another go. When we eventually did get to the right spot and reported to Flying Control they were highly amused, having been tracking us round and round the aerodrome on their radar. After being used to no lights except the odd Chance Light overseas, the Drem system at Chivenor and all the little coloured lights, complicated dispersals and real runways seemed like Blackpool with full illuminations.

'Soon after we arrived, No 14 Squadron turned up from the Middle East, where they had been flying Marauders, and were now to convert to Wellingtons; while around Christmas time No 407 Squadron's Canadians arrived with a series of beat-ups designed to impress. The Wellingtons of all three squadrons operating from Chivenor around Christmas 1944 were all painted white with dark grey (plain) upper surfaces. On ops we carried overload tanks fitted into the bomb bays, and six DCs in the outer bays. As most ops were performed by night, we were equipped with Leigh Lights. The Leigh Light/radar combination worked very well indeed provided that the SE operator gave a good running commentary and the pilot acted upon it, and was also capable of working out in his head

Above: **Wimpy Mk VIII, with ASV Mk II aerial display, under-wing array, and armed tail and nose gun turrets for day torpedo role.** */Author's Collection*

Above right: **Wellington XIV (Leigh Light), NB829 'O', of No 36 Squadron at Chivenor, late 1944. Fitted with ASV Mk 3 radar, Leigh Light, GEE, Loran (some), nose, tail and mid-ship machine guns, six 250lb depth charges, plus the usual variety of pyrotechnic stores; the Wimpy XIV was a veritable flying Christmas tree!**/*G. E. Jones*

Right: **Anti-sub base. Vertical view of RAF Chivenor, Devon, in 1944-45 era.**/*J. Rounce*

Above: **Wellington IV (LL), HF113/G, 'P-Peter' flying off the estuary of Taw-Torridge, west of Chivenor, 1944. Note radar scanner 'chin' housing, and under-belly Leigh Light (retracted).**/*J. Rounce*

the necessary course adjustments to achieve an interception over a moving target.

'The idea was as follows. Radar picked up a target, usually at approximately eight or nine miles, although this could be as much as 20 or as little as three miles, depending on the set, weather conditions, and operator. If the target looked promising, or had not been previously investigated, the pilot and rest of the crew were informed over the intercomm. If it was decided to have a look-see, dashing about commenced. The nav went amidships to lower the light, usually doing a bit of swearing as this meant upsetting his charts and other paraphernalia. He then came back and handed a position for the W/T operator to send to Group in the form of a flash report, this being very brief and consisting of a certain group in the Aircraft Reporting Code, with a position and time. Meantime the second pilot went forward and laid down in the nose to operate the light; the controls in the nose enabled the light to be swung from side to side and also up and down to a maximum of five degrees in each direction. The nav then came forward and kneeled over the second pilot to work the single .303in Browning in the nose. The rear gunner cocked his guns and was ready to have a go when the time came, and to report results.

'During all this time the radar op was continuing his talking, giving target distance and position in degrees right or left. The pilot lost height until at one mile from target he'd be at 50ft, and at three-quarters of a mile the light was switched on. If all had gone well the target was well and truly lit up and dead ahead. It usually worked out. The pilot then dropped his DCs visually. Radar kept up his chat once over the target to enable the aircraft to be brought round for a second go. Obviously the further away the target was picked up in the first place, the more time we had for getting things organised. At 50ft at night and probably over a rough sea the Wimpy was a

fairly big aeroplane to play about with – 86ft wing-span – and, thinking back, I have come to the conclusion that we should have been rather more frightened than we were. I can only suppose we were all so busy that it didn't occur to us that we might easily fly straight into the drink. A radio altimeter with coloured lights blinking enabled the pilot to stay at 50ft.

'Chivenor – known to all as the "Happidrome" – was a good station, close to Barnstaple and not far from Ilfracombe. It was the only station I ever met that had an "Ops Canteen" in the Flying Control which, apart from flying meals, used to have a churn of fresh milk and a large box of raisins every morning at 10 o'clock – eat and drink as much as you like – and all for free. The winter 1944-45 was cold – we were told it never snowed in Devon, but it did that winter, and in February the runways had a foot of snow on them. It took the whole station, including the CO, two days to shovel the main runway clear. Then, no sooner had we managed to get one Wimpy away on an op than it thawed – rapidly. At one end of the short runway stood the church, which one passed within feet when using said runway. It had a red warning light on top – resulting in a few ribald comments by the crews whenever they flew by . . . A lot of the crews' spare time was spent in Barnstaple, and the last train to Wrafton left at 10.30pm – always very full, dark, and ideal for that last cuddle with the current WAAF girl-friend. The fare was about twopence (old money) and the 10.30 "Special" was very much a part of the Chivenor scene then.

'We used to fly every third or fourth night on patrols, but during the day we did a fair amount of practice homing on ships and other aircraft, and air firing against towed targets. On one such occasion we had been practising homings on a submarine in Cardigan Bay and having finished playing we

Above: **Wellington GR XIV NB773, RW-D of No 36 Squadron at Benbecula in May 1945. 'Holding it up' is WO Gordon Jones.**/*G. Jones*

fired a Very Light to let the sub know we were going home. The Very pistol in a Wimpy was above the head of the W/T operator, half-in and half-outside the fuselage. Some of the red-hot cartridge filling must have fallen back onto the top of the fuselage fabric, because I was standing looking out over the second pilot's shoulder and happened to turn round to the WOP, when I noticed the top of the fuselage around the Very pistol was burning away quite merrily. If you've ever tried to put out a fire in an upward direction with an extinguisher designed to operate downwards, you'll know it's not easy. We managed, however, though it caused a fair amount of alarm; while the extinguisher contents did not improve the W/T set or the operator's log books etc. (This happened to our crew once before, at OTU, when we landed all aglow, piled out, and watched the aeroplane really go up in smoke.)

'Benbecula (in the Hebrides) was the squadron's next home. We flew up from Chivenor in March 1945 and lost one aircraft on the way somehow. Benbecula was a bleak, windswept place and we were the only squadron there. Things got back to a real squadron life where everything centred around the Mess. Our ops from there were again anti-U-boat patrols and daylight convoy escorts. The U-boats were now using snorts (Schnorkel tubes) which made life more difficult. I only saw one; I was in the turret and the weather was foul. By the time we had turned to make a run it had gone completely. Most of our patrols were carried out at heights from 600ft to about 2,000, according to the weather. We were still at Benbecula when the war in Europe ended and, along with most other squadrons in Coastal, carried on flying for some time after, bringing in U-boats that had given themselves up – Blue Line patrols, as these were known. I can remember on VE night everyone got very happy – including some of the boys who

managed to set fire to the guard-room roof. By then I'd been with No 36 Squadron for over 12 months, flying with the same crew – a long time with just one unit then.'

In May 1942 Coastal Command was 'loaned' several Bomber Command units, including No 304 (Silesian) Squadron; a Wellington bomber unit comprised almost wholly of Polish air and ground crews, which had just completed its first full year of operations over Germany. Based initially at Tiree, No 304 Squadron left the barren island on 13 June 1942, flying south to Dale, South Wales, where its operational zone mainly entailed patrols over the Bay of Biscay, hunting for U-boats. This meant flying for many hours in broad daylight within interception range of the various German fighter units based around the Biscay coastline; relatively slow, clumsy targets for the swift Junkers Ju88s, Focke Wulf Fw190s, or Messerschmitts constantly prowling above the Bay.

On 16 September 1942, Wellington 'E-for-Ela of No 304 Squadron was airborne at 0930 and within five minutes was setting out on its 140-mile leg to the Biscay area; briefed for a 'routine' U-boat search. The navigator, Flt Lt Minakowski, takes up the story.

'As we approached position "A" at 1612, six aircraft appeared; one starboard, three to port and two far astern. The sky was cloudless and the weather fine, with visibility between 25-30 miles from our altitude of 1,500ft. Flg Off Stanislas Targowski, our pilot, descended to 500ft when the aircraft were sighted and, when we identified them as Ju88s, jettisoned our depth charges and went further down to 50ft.'

The enemy fighters closed in rapidly. At 1615 three Ju88s bore in from the port front quarter, one after another, and Targowski threw the Wellington into violent evasive manoeuvres, almost dipping the wings into

61

Above: Big Brother. The Vickers Warwick V (PN698 illustrated) was too late to see operational service during the war, but served with Coastal units in the immediate postwar period. The GR5 carried Leigh Light, full radar and other anti-submarine equipment; yet achieved a loaded top speed of more than 250mph with a crew of six./*G. Jones* /*D. Nicholson*

Centre right: Warwick GR V, PN811, of No 179 Squadron, in full 1945 Coastal Command livery. /*Author's Collection*

Bottom right: The Warwick ASR I version – BV301 is illustrated – built for ASR duties specifically, in which capacity it served as the equipment of some ten Coastal squadrons. In this view can be seen an airborne lifeboat slung under the bomb bay. /*Ministry of Aircraft Production, Crown copyright*

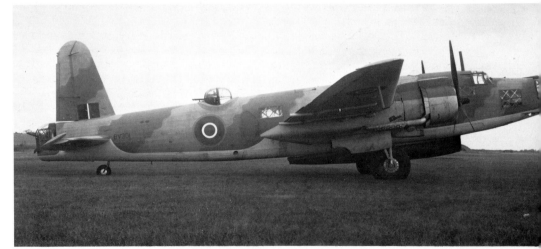

Above: **Wellington NZ-Q of 304 (Polish) Squadron, at Syerston, 1941.**
/*via W. Baguley*

the sea. Each time a Junkers came in, he turned to face it head-on, thereby presenting the smallest possible target. Both front and rear gunners opened fire as the first Ju88 came on and hit one of them and saw it fall into the sea. The wireless operator, after transmitting a signal to base about the attack and the aircraft's location, manned the beam gun. Minakowski's report continues:

'Two Junkers – those originally farthest away – now closed in from starboard, passed us and then attacked. They nearly succeeded. As one attacked on the starboard beam, our Wellington turned head-on towards him and was struck by cannon shells and a machine-gun burst. One of the petrol tanks was damaged and the cabin was filled with smoke from the explosions. All our guns were banging away furiously. Another Hun was hit and pieces fell off him as he turned towards France with smoke streaming out of his starboard engine. Shortly after this a crash resounded in the Wellington and dense smoke filled the fuselage. There were no fumes, however, and nobody was wounded. Some clouds appeared on the horizon just then and we made for them.

'Two fighters now attacked us time after time from astern. Both were hit by our gunners who greeted them with accurate fire as they got within close range. Thereafter the enemy's attacks were half-hearted. The clouds were by now much closer, about 1,500ft up, so Targowski made for them at full speed.

He reached them safely, and we finally broke away from the enemy. We fixed our position and informed base we would land at Portreath in Cornwall, owing to fuel shortage. The petrol in the starboard tank had all leaked out, and the auxiliary oil-delivery tank was damaged. We landed at 1750, having been airborne for 8hr 20min. None of us was hurt.'

Wellington 'E-for-Ela' had clearly made its last sortie; the damage was widespread. Sustaining nearly 40 bullet or cannon strikes, the starboard petrol tank had a six-inch square hole; the auxiliary oil tank was damaged; a jagged three feet by six feet hole had been ripped out in the wing fabric; wing ribs were damaged; airscrew spinners, engine nacelles, astro-dome, aerial, and the length of the fuselage all bore strikes and ruptures. Exactly one month later, on 16 October 1942, Flg Off Stanislas Targowski set off in high spirits on yet another trip over the notorious Biscay. That morning he had received his first letter from his wife, still in Poland – his first since 1939 – while only two hours after he left the squadron received notification of an award of the DFC for Targowski, and immediately set about preparing a celebration party for his return. The squadron waited in vain – somewhere over the Bay that day Targowski and his crew, including four of 'E-Ela's crew on 16 September, were shot into the sea by the Luftwaffe.

Queen of the 'Boats

Of some 50 types of aircraft used by Coastal Command during the years 1939-45, only one was actually employed on first-line operational duties from the first to the last day of the war – the Short Sunderland flying boat. Last in a long proud line of flying boat designs in RAF service, the Sunderland was without question the finest 'boat ever used by the Service; it was the Queen. Resulting from a 1933 Air Ministry Specification, the first prototype Sunderland, K4774, made its first-ever flight at Rochester, Kent on 16 October 1937; while the first Sunderland to enter RAF service was L2159 on 28 May 1938, which was flown to Seletar, Singapore to join No 230 Squadron on 22 June 1938. At the outbreak of war in September 1939, No 210 Squadron had six Sunderlands on strength, while No 204 Squadron, based at Mount Batten, Plymouth began receiving its Sunderlands from July 1939. Four of No 210 Squadron's pilots, who flew Sunderlands on operations during the first month of war, were Australians from an RAAF detachment

which had arrived in England in July tasked with receiving and flying back a complement of Sunderlands to Australia for RAAF use. In the event, this Australian 'detachment', based at Pembroke Dock, was enlarged in RAAF and RAF personnel to become the nucleus of No 10 Squadron, RAAF. On 3 January 1940 the Aussie Sunderland squadron was officially taken under the aegis of 15 Group, Coastal Command, and was declared operational with effect from 1 February; flying its first operational sortie five days later.

By August 1945 a total of 20 RAF squadrons had employed Sunderlands on operations in virtually every war zone from Britain to the Burman jungle; apart from several Dominion units. Factory production of the Sunderland continued until 14 June 1946, but the RAF continued flying Sunderlands in a myriad of roles and duties until 20 May 1959; the date of the ultimate Sunderland flight bearing RAF roundels. Even thereafter individual Sunderlands flew with various foreign services; while today, standing proudly opposite

Below: **Sunderland I, L2163, 'G' of No 210 Squadron, early 1940. It later served with No 10 Squadron RAAF, and by January 1942 was with No 228 Squadron.**/*IWM*

Above: RAF Mount Batten, Plymouth, viewed here before 1939, which became a premier flying boat and marine craft base for several decades.
/via H. Seymour

Left: Be it ever so 'umble . . . SS *Manela*, the floating 'home' for a long succession of Coastal crews, from Iceland to Singapore (as here), throughout the war. Like its sister ship SS *Dumana*, the *Manela* was an ex-British India Steamship Company vessel, equipped throughout with the company's crockery et al.
/C. Lock

Below: Qui vive. A No 201 Squadron Sunderland skipper checking a possible target in the distance./*IWM*

the main entrance to the Royal Air Force Museum at Hendon, Sunderland GR5, ML824, which saw brief operational wartime service with Nos 201 and 330 Squadrons, remains as a permanent reminder of the design's superlative and extensive service.

Life as a member of a Sunderland crew was in many ways unique in RAF circles and experience. Whereas almost all other types of aircraft crews used their aircraft for operations, test flying and, occasionally, communications, Sunderland crews looked upon their 'boat as virtually board and lodging when away from their base station. Certainly the main necessities of life were provided for in the Sunderland, with its own water and food supplies catered for in the primitive galley, while ample space was available for rest bunks and other relaxation facilities. This individuality extended to the operational scene, where – as with most Coastal Command captains – the skipper and his crew were essentially 'on their own' once airborne for an over-sea patrol. Once 'on the way' the Sunderland, its crew and armament, combined to make a fighting 'whole'; and the skipper had the highest degree of autocratic decision within the limits of his general pre-briefing for the sortie. Flexibility, adaptability, instant initiative – all were normal and necessary to any Coastal Command crew; in the Sunderland could be added a better-than-average ration of independence.

Despite its mammoth proportions and ruggedness in structural design, the Sunderland was not, however, intended for operation in heavy seas or oceanic waters. Its true element was in coastal waters and sheltered harbours. For example, the hull planing surface skin was of merely $\frac{1}{16}$ in thick treated alloy metal. It speaks volumes, therefore, of the cool courage of the many Sunderland captains who deliberately attempted to land in wild Atlantic swells, trying to retrieve ditched air crews. A high proportion of such rescue operations were indeed successful – often in spite of an express Command order forbidding open-sea landings without specific permission. Tragically, too many such attempts ended swiftly in disaster – the angry ocean smashing the giant metal boat to pieces, with an almost contemptuous ease. Perhaps it was that very spirit of individuality engendered by all Coastal operations which initiated such risky ventures; more likely it was simply an extension of the tightly-knit bond of comradeship which bound all crews to any fellow crew in mortal danger . . .

Not that the vast majority of Coastal Command operations were filled with activity, excitement, or blood-heating action. Contrary to the impressions gained from many accounts of the air-sea warfare of 1939-45, the huge bulk of Coastal Command's oper-

Above: **Grub up! A 1940 Sunderland 'chef' dishes up an in-flight meal. Note airman at left still wearing his prewar 'dog-collar'-style tunic.**/*Topical Press*

ations were usually comprised of hour upon monotonous hour of watching an endless vista of empty water, without even a sniff of a U-boat or Luftwaffe opposition. Nevertheless, the vital need for constant alertness remained; if action came, it always called for almost split-second decisions with equally instant follow-up action. Such action was rare in most crews' experience. A more typical Sunderland sortie is exemplified by the account given by Flt Lt Jack Sumner, skipper of a No 423 Squadron RCAF Sunderland crew based at Castle Archdale in late 1942:

'The time, 0030. The batman taps the sleeping skipper on the shoulder. "Time to get up, sir, briefing's at one-thirty, take-off three-thirty." (Batmen could seldom tell the time in Service officialese . . .). A few hours before, the weather had looked anything but promising. The sky was heavy with a low overcast, and rain was pelting down – real "scrub" weather. Bed felt especially comfortable and warm as the batman shuffled off to wake the other officers. Nonetheless . . .

'Sleepy-eyed aircrew stumble through a drenching downpour to their Messes. Breakfast consists of porridge, bacon and egg, tea or coffee, and "lashings of toast and marmalade". "Looks like a really long stooge this time", some pre-informed flight engineer remarks. Engineers had a talent for ferretting out the gen about forthcoming ops before anyone else. "Almost seven hundred miles out! They'd better have those petrol tanks good and full or there'll be a lot of us in the drink waiting for the air-sea rescue types."

'By briefing time the clouds have gone and the sky is a mass of stars. A strong wind has picked up, which means head-winds on the way out. Covering one wall of the briefing room is an Atlantic area map which itself looks as big as an ocean. Lines of ribbon run out from British ports to code-lettered sea positions that represent the latest reported positions of convoys in-bound from America. Just beyond 25deg West is a miniature submarine. "That's where you're going," announces the Operations Officer, pointing to the U-boat marker. "Americans patrolling that area yesterday came on a pack of subs. They attacked them but we don't know what the results were. As you can see from the chart, there's a convoy in the vicinity, but your job is those submarines. You'll get the weather conditions from the met man."

'The weather-merchant is far from happy. Only the urgency of the situation, he admits, permits the operation in the first place. The weather overhead is purely a local condition. Information from the Atlantic is so vague that he cannot predict with any accuracy. There are several fronts out there, but their movements are indefinite. "If you're lucky you may return under conditions just as they are now" – and he adds, "or it may get thick."

'After a few words from the squadron commander (Wg Cdr F. J. Rump), the air crews leave the briefing room. Sumner's navigator, WO Harry Parliament, is loaded down with maps and charts. The second pilot, Plt Off George Holley, carries two orange-coloured metal boxes housing Gertie and George, homing pigeons which will be released if the Sunderland is forced down at sea. At the docks crews board motor boats which take them to their flying yachts moored well out in the lake. There the rest of the crew of "J" awaits them – Plt Off Art Mountford, Sgts Jack Kelly, Hal Hutchinson, Phil Marshall, J. B. Horsburgh and A. J. Lunn. They have been in the aircraft all night, having slept aboard. Mountford is busy making tea in the galley. There is still time before take-off, and the crew sit around the table in the wardroom, chatting the minutes away.

'Suddenly the skipper looks at his watch, heaves himself to his feet, and gives the order to douse cigarettes and the oil heater. It's time to start up. In quick succession four Pegasus power-plants kick to life, then merge into an unsynchronised roar. The big 'boat moves towards the flare path – a row of lights bobbing on the water – guided by a dinghy-borne airman flashing an Aldis lamp. Both pilots make their pre-take-off checks, the crew get into their take-off positions, and presently the ship is trimmed and ready to go. Then, throttles opening wide in an angry crescendo, the Sunderland gathers momentum, pulls itself up on to the step, and is soon moving over the lake at express train speed. Sumner brings back the control column in one smooth movement, with a slight jerk, and "J-Jig" gets airborne.

'But the operation isn't yet under way. Before reaching its patrol area "Jig" is recalled because of threatening weather at base. It returns to the mooring place and the crew awaits another order to go. This comes sooner than expected, and the routine begins all over again. This time it's a convoy escort. The briefing is much like the previous one, except that one of the U-boats has been definitely sunk and another two probably destroyed by escort surface vessels. But a pack of them are still shadowing the convoy and it must have aerial protection – it's that simple.

'Taking off again in darkness the Sunderland, soon after first light, reaches the area where it is to pick up the convoy. Sumner and Holley scan the ocean for sign of a ship. Mountford is glued to his wireless set, Parliament checks and rechecks his navigation, Kelly swings his mid-upper turret slowly back and forth. The wireless operator calls the captain on the intercomm and gives

Below: **The mobile bomb rack of No 10 Squadron RAAF Sunderland, loaded here with four 250lb AS bombs, in the extended 'attack' position.**/*IWM*

him a radio bearing on the convoy. A course alteration is made to starboard and soon the long lines of ships are in sight. The Sunderland begins to circle the convoy just within visual range. The armament of those ships carried quite a sting and it was considered unwise to venture too close to them until they'd sent out a recognition signal. It wasn't unusual for such ships to shoot first and ask questions afterwards!

'The message of recognition is received, followed by a second message giving a bearing on a suspected submarine well to starboard of the convoy. Everybody aboard the Sunderland perks up. Even if they don't see one, at least they'll have the satisfaction of knowing that their presence is keeping one of the foe out of striking range. The circling goes on and on . . . A welcome break in the monotony comes with the call to lunch. The crew retires in shifts to the wardroom to partake of thick steaks with potatoes and turnips, and a "dessert" of bread and jam. The next meal, tea, will feature fried egg sandwiches. Time passes – slowly – the monotony grows. Everyone is wishing the patrol would hurry up and end.

'As if in deference to their wishes the alarm siren shrieks and red warning lights flash. "The skip's spotted something!" Hutchinson shouts as he heads towards the bomb racks. As he and another crew man pull down the side flaps of the bomb bay, and press the button that moves the depth charges out on a track to their position on the lower surface of the wing, Sumner banks as tightly as possible and dives at full throttle in the direction of something long and black in the distance. The thing – it's a sub all right – appears to be five miles away, but distances are deceptive over water. Uppermost in each man's mind is the

question, "Will it see us and submerge before we can attack?" The answer comes only seconds later, when the alarmed enemy crash-dives to safety. The vicinity around the sub's vanishing act is carefully scrutinised, but any attempt to depth-charge now would be nothing but the wildest stab in the dark – the raider may have beetled-off in any direction. "Bring in the bombs", orders the skipper, and the load of high explosive returns to its stowage in the fuselage.

'Now the circling begins anew, but the patrol period is soon over. A signal to that effect is sent to one of the escort destroyers. The Sunderland turns for home . . .'

If Jack Sumner's sortie was only too typical of so many Coastal skippers, a patrol just over a year later by another No 423 Squadron Sunderland crew illustrates graphically what could happen on the rare occasion of pure action. Flt Lt F. G. Fellows, RCAF was skipper of Sunderland DD826, AB-A on 24 April 1944, engaged in a creeping-line-ahead search for U-boats during the afternoon. Visibility, for a change, was unlimited, and Fellows spotted what he thought was a wake. Increasing speed to 140kts, while his second pilot trained his binoculars on the spot and confirmed that it was a U-boat, Fellows soon made out the definite shape of a surfaced submarine about 16 miles dead ahead. At five miles range the U-boat evidently spotted Fellows' Sunderland and, instead of crash-diving, began evasive manoeuvring attempting to keep its stern towards the approaching flying boat, and meanwhile bringing into play its flak guns.

Following each manoeuvre of the sub, Fellows eventually got to a position up-sun and then bore in on a straight attack run. At

Above and left: Wg Cdr John Barrett, DFC, (far left) and his crew of Sunderland ML778, Z/201, prior to the final war patrol of 3/4 June 1945; and (second view) *Z-Zebra* at low height over its convoy charges. At one minute after midnight on 4 June, when some 500 miles SW of Ireland, *Zebra* received the order to 'Cease patrol' with appropriate naval thanks./*IWM*

1,200yd the Sunderland's four fixed nose guns and twin nose turret guns opened up, smothering the conning tower flak crews and churning up a fury of plumes of water and spray around the tower itself; so effectively that flak from the submarine ceased at 300yd range. The Sunderland had suffered numerous hits as it made its run-in, but Fellows kept the aircraft rock-steady, tracking directly over the still-surfaced U-boat, and dropping six depth charges at 60ft intervals. As the rear gunner with his guns fully depressed saw the sub enter his sights, he pressed the firing controls – and there was a violent explosion. The blast appeared to have been No 4 depth charge detonating prematurely on striking the sub's hull.

The blast created pure havoc in the Sunderland. Every item not nailed down became 'airborne', with floorboards, crockery, IFF set, crew and some loose eggs, being thrown around in a gyrating mix. The rear gunner was knocked unconscious, the wireless operator thrown from his astro-dome perch and knocked dizzy, all electrical circuits rendered unserviceable, the R/T cable cut, wing seams burst open, and the port flap damaged seriously. Apart from damage to the rear turret, the whole airframe was twisted, and the elevators almost put out of function; while the rear-facing camera's leads were severed. Now extremely tail-heavy, the Sunderland tried to climb and, though trimmed to full nose-heavy, it took all the skill and combined strength of Fellows and his second pilot to keep 'A-Able' flying straight and level.

A few seconds after the depth charges went into the sea, an ugly brownish pool appeared just behind the U-boat, which was stern down and listing steadily. It took some three minutes for Fellows to regain reasonable control of his aircraft but he immediately struggled round for a second attack. In that interval the U-boat disappeared from view, leaving just a spreading patch of oil but no wreckage. Searching the sea carefully Fellows found no further evidence of results, and on return to base merely claimed the submarine as 'Damaged'. Later, confirmation came in that his victim had been the U-311 which had sunk with all hands.

Dudley Marrows was an Australian, born in Bendigo in 1917, and engaged in accountancy when the war started in Europe. Forsaking double-entry columns for an aircraft control column, he soon joined the RAAF, and on arriving in England saw his initial operational service with No 201 Squadron RAF in Coastal Command, flying Sunderlands. By the summer of 1943 'Dud' had joined his fellow Aussies in No 461 Squadron RAAF,

still piloting Sunderlands from Pembroke Dock. On 30 July that year he was patrolling the Spanish coastal waters – yet another apparently unfruitful sortie, like every other sortie he'd flown in the past year. With several hundred operational hours marked up in his log book, Marrows had yet to even see a U-boat, let alone attack one. He had long ago resigned himself to this fact of Coastal ops, and simply continued to plod across the ocean watching water, though always retaining just a faint hope of one day having a go at at least one U-boat before the war was over. The patrol had been uneventful – a few suspiciously peaceful fishing smacks going about their timeless trade (though he knew that these innocuous-looking smacks might well be forward listening posts for the nearby land-based Luftwaffe Jagdstaffeln) – and he was about to turn for home when his wireless operator reported a signal from a Liberator, giving details of some surfaced U-boats. The fix given was some 200 miles away from Marrows, so he figured they were too far for him to have any hope of joining in any attack, and therefore continued his course for home.

A few minutes later, however, the wireless operator spoke to Marrows again, 'Message from Group, Skipper. We're to go to 45° 42' North, 11° West where the U-boat pack is still'. Still unconvinced privately that he'd ever reach the surfaced subs in time, Marrows nevertheless obeyed his orders and swung the Sunderland onto the new course. His fuel wasn't too plentiful, now, they had already flown half a normal patrol, but with a careful watch on the dials he should still manage it. The new track was northwards anyway – his homeward course – and he had enough juice for a normal return leg, plus a drop to spare. Any action en route would drastically reduce the odds of reaching base in terms of fuel, but Marrows was philosophical – he'd cross that bridge when (and if) he came to it. Two hours later a crew member yelled, 'Three destroyers, starboard bow, 15 miles'. As Marrows closed the range to 12 miles of the three vessels dead ahead of him, his first pilot, peering through his binoculars, said, 'They're not destroyers, they're U-boats!' Marrows' heart leapt, excitement surged within him, and he slipped all four engines into rich mixture for top boost – to hell with petrol conservation! He warned the crew to take up action stations and to prepare the 'boat for trouble.

As the range closed to five miles, Marrows could see clearly that the air-sea battle was already well under way. In the water were three surfaced U-boats (U-461, U-462, and U-504), each of which was obeying the latest order from their high commander, Dönitz, to stay surfaced and fight it out with any aerial opposition. The sky around them was black with flak bursts, testimony to the submarine commanders' determination to adhere to that order. Wheeling around and through this wall of fire were several aircraft. The Liberator ('O' of No 53 Squadron, Flg Off W. Irving) which had first reported the U-boats, was still trying to penetrate the flak curtain; while also circulating, trying to figure a good way of getting at the subs was another Liberator (No 19 Squadron, USN) and a Halifax (No 502 Squadron, Flg Off Hensow, a Dutchman). The flak had already punished another Halifax ('B' of No 502 Squadron, Flt Lt Jenson) for his attempt to bomb, and Jenson was on his way home, nursing a crippled aircraft; while a Catalina, called to the scene too, had flown off to summon a surface group of destroyers.

As Marrows 'joined the circuit' around the attack zone he watched Hensow take his Halifax in low for a straight bomb run, then deliberately make three more runs from 3,000ft; releasing one of his three special 600lb anti-submarine bombs on each of the latter runs. One of the Dutchman's bombs found its mark, close to U-462, crippling the sub and causing it finally to stop. Marvelling privately at the Halifax skipper's blind courage in deliberately plunging through such a wall of fire, Marrows decided it was time he had a go. Dropping one wing-tip, he turned the Sunderland towards the U-boats and, at 1,000ft height, roared in; only to quickly realise that the flak was just too hot to offer any real chance of success this way. He swung out of his run and circuited again, pondering how best to slip through the curtain of fire.

Just then the American Liberator's pilot came through to him on the R/T, suggesting that they both attack together and thereby 'split' the flak between them. Accordingly, both aircraft, 400yd apart, started their attack runs. The U-boats promptly turned broadside to the aircraft and put up yet another devastating hail of fire. Both aircraft throttled back and pulled away to think again. This time Irving, in Liberator 'O' of No 53 Squadron, led the 'charge' of all three aircraft. Followed closely by the American Liberator, Irving dived towards the trio of subs, refusing to baulk at the combined flak being concentrated upon him. Marrows realised that here was his chance to sneak in virtually 'unobserved'. Ramming all four throttles through the 'gate' he swung the Sunderland over fiercely and roared in a mile behind the Liberators, fast and low.

The Sunderland got within 1,000yd before the flak gunners switched their aim towards it. Cannon shells and bright tracers hammered through the flying boat's starboard wing and splashed along its flanks. Plunging down almost to the sea surface, Marrows held tight and nosed straight into the teeth of the fire. In the nose turret the gunner opened up, sweeping the port U-boat's flak crew overboard in a withering hail of bullets. The sub's conning tower loomed almost monstrously in Marrow's vision dead ahead, then missed his wing float by mere inches as the Sunderland thundered overhead. In the same second Marrows let go a stick of seven depth charges in a line across and just forward of the U-boat's superstructure – then ran straight through the fire of the other subs' guns. Pulling back on his control column with every ounce of his considerable strength, Marrows jinked and screwed his way up and out of the murderous crossfire, seeking calmer air.

Behind him an immense eruption engulfed his target – and the U-boat snapped in the middle like a rotten twig. Marrows, still wholly intent on his 'kill', reached height, turned as tightly as possible, and headed back towards his chosen target sub. Tracers and shells still flaked around him, but below he could see a brilliant red-orange pool of oil, wreckage and scum, with some 30 U-boat crew members dazedly, frantically trying to grab anything which floated. Marrows took in the whole scene in a second, then swept over the survivors fast and low – and dropped a dinghy near to the struggling sailors. Enemy or not, they were brave men; it was the time for mercy. Climbing again, Marrows swiftly checked out his crew for any injuries or damage, found that he still had one depth charge available on the under-wing rack, and looked around for a target to use it against.

The only surviving U-boat, still undamaged, was now heading for the open Atlantic, so Marrows turned towards it, intent on using his last shot as effectively as possible. The sky around him suddenly filled with flak; thick, almost inpenetrable. Marrows couldn't believe that one U-boat could throw up so much iron; then realised that he was in the middle of a purely sea battle – the 2nd Escort Group,

Above: **Flt Lt Dudley Marrows, DSO, DFC, RAAF, who served with No 461 Squadron, RAAF (Sunderlands) and sank U-461 on 30 July 1943.** */Australian War Memorial*

summoned by the Catalina, had arrived on the scene and was pouring shells at the sole remaining U-boat (U-502). Almost with relief, Marrows abandoned his intended attack and climbed into clear air. He watched the other aircraft put down marine markers on the locations of the wreckage of the two sunken U-boats, then flew over the RN Escort Group, signalling the news of the sinkings and the positions of the surviving German crew members. 'Next stop, home', he said cheerfully to his crew, only to receive the calm voice of his engineer, 'We haven't enough petrol to reach home, skipper.'

With little alternative, Marrows set course for the Scilly Isles – with luck and careful judgement they *might* just scrape in there; if not, at least they wouldn't need to ditch *too* far from civilisation. While the Sunderland settled onto its latest course, with the pilots and engineer anxiously watching the instruments and quietly calculating their remaining airborne endurance; Marrows' other crew men chattered excitedly over the intercomm;

Left: **Weary Willie. ZM-W of No 201 Squadron on 28 October 1941, above a choppy sea surface. Though festooned with radar 'stickleback' aerials on the fuselage, and Yagi underwing antennae, this Sunderland still retains the two dorsal gun hatches.**
/RAF Kinloss/No 201 Squadron, RAF

Below left: **The never-ending task of maintenance by the ever-loyal ground crews, exemplified here on a No 201 Squadron Sunderland at Castle Archdale./IWM**

Below: **Pee-Dee – the RAF abbreviation for Pembroke Dock flying boat base, in Wales; a station from which many Sunderland crews flew throughout 1939-45 and later./Author's Collection**

reaction to the acutely intense drama behind them now found release. Then Marrows almost jumped in his seat as the voice of his nose gunner yelled, 'U-boat on starboard bow!' 'Forty degrees starboard, one and a half miles!!' Marrows couldn't believe it – a year of seeing sweet Fanny Adams, now *four* sightings all in a single patrol! His befuddled mind took in the thought – then cleared instantly. 'I'm going straight in! Get that depth charge out!'

Going straight down from 2,000ft in an unswerving dive, the Sunderland closed on its unsuspecting target at 1,000yd and the front guns opened up, spraying the sub's decks. As the German crew on deck realised what was happening they manned the submarine's flak guns and began pumping shells at the flying boat as it loomed large. Marrows prepared to set his controls for a fast pull-out once over his target – but found he couldn't budge the controls. The aircraft continued downwards with Marrows fighting the controls, his feet against the dials, exerting every ounce of

muscle power in his attempt to bring the Sunderland out of its dive. The Sunderland's nose inched up, reluctantly, and swept over the U-boat so low that the German gunners ducked their heads. Pushing the bomb release button, Marrows got no response – the bomb gear traversing motor had seized and was on fire. As the engineer dowsed the small fire Marrows and his first pilot fought to get their aircraft into a climb and finally succeeded. It was the last straw for Marrows. With dud bomb gear, little petrol, and now (apparently) flak-damaged controls, he figured he'd had a busy day; it was time to go home . . .

As he left the last U-boat to its own devices, Marrows checked around his cockpit – and then realised what had caused that last, almost fatal controls' 'failure'; he'd accidentally engaged 'George', the automatic pilot, his sleeve operating the lever, during the hasty action against his last target. With a sigh of relief, he returned the controls to 'manual' and concentrated on trying to reach land and safety. By meticulous balancing of all factors, he finally made it; landing in the channel outside St Mary's in the Scillies. The petrol tanks were to all intents dry by the time he cut motors.

Confirmation of Dud Marrows' U-boat sinking came into the squadron later. By a sheer fluke of coincidence, Sunderland 'U' of No 461 Squadron had sunk U-boat, U-461 . . . Little more than two weeks later, on 16 September, Marrows and his crew were attacked by six Junkers Ju88s off the Spanish coast on what was to have been Marrows' ultimate operational sortie with No 461 Squadron prior to being shipped back to Australia. The fight was a bloody one, with the Sunderland damaging every Junkers in turn until, cut to ribbons, with wounded men aboard, Marrows was forced to ditch his crippled flying boat, after an hour of desperate combat against vastly superior odds. The faithful Sunderland stayed afloat long enough for Marrows and his crew to gather provisions and launch dinghies; then as the dinghies left it, the aircraft slid into the depths – almost with dignity (as one crew man described it). They were found by a Leigh Light Catalina in the early hours of the next morning and by mid-morning a destroyer group hove into view and retrieved them from the sea. By yet another coincidence it was the same 2nd Destroyer Group which had finished off the action of 30 July, and its commander Capt F. J. Walker, CB, DSO presented Dudley Marrows with the life-jacket and escape gear worn by Kapitänleutnant Stiebler, commander of Marrow's victim, U-461. Several weeks later Flt Lt Dudley Marrows, DSO, DFC, RAAF went back to Australia, saw further service with No 40 Squadron, RAAF, and survived the war.

Below: Liberator GR IIIs of No 120 Squadron at Aldergrove, near Belfast – an aerodrome derived from a 1917-18 airfield, which itself was first suggested in 1912. Nearest aircraft are FK228, M and FL933, O. /IWM

Lib Skipper

John Luker transferred from the Army in April 1941 for pilot training, taking his ITW at Aberystwyth, EFTS at Sealand and completing his flying training at 5 FTS, Grantham, being awarded his 'wings' on 12 November 1941. For the next year he flew as a staff pilot at 1(C) OTU, Silloth, and then undertook an OTU course – at Silloth – on Hudsons; gathering his crew of three by the end of the course in January 1943, and being posted to No 120 Squadron at Ballykelly, Northern Ireland – to fly Liberators!

'We stayed together to form the nucleus of a new Liberator crew forming under Flg Off Dennis Webber – I had, of course, to do a stint as second pilot, the normal procedure for Lib squadrons. We soon moved to Aldergrove and thence to Reykjavik, Iceland in April 1943. For our flight we were armed and briefed for an anti-sub sweep – our first operation as a new crew, now seven in number and soon to be eight. No 120 Squadron then was flying Liberator IIIs, but we also had one or two Mark Is still operational, these latter having four 20mm cannons firing forward from under the main fuselage. We were a day squadron and our main task was westward into the Atlantic on convoy escorts and, sometimes, anti-submarine patrols. Normal patrols lasted 15 hr.

'Our first full operation from Reykjavik saw us returning in foul weather and being diverted to the US base at Meeks Field (now Keflavik) temporarily. We flew off for Reykjavik soon after and our total flying hours for this trip amounted to 17hr 40 min. There was little if any darkness in Iceland in midsummer – conversely in winter, of course – and the whole 17hr 40min was entered in my log book under "day" flying.

'I also recorded a few flights in the Liberator I. I remember a senior pilot on the squadron moaning constantly about this particular Mark of Lib, but "gallantly" offering to fly a Mk I to save the rest of us embarrassment. He was the only pilot (as I remember) who thus virtually had his "own" aircraft, because with such lengthy operations and the need for major inspections to be done still in Ballykelly it was impossible to allocate a particular aircraft to just one crew. One day, however, this senior pilot went sick and we replaced him on an op and flew his much-grumbled-about Mk I – it was a marvellous aeroplane, and the best Lib I ever flew in! Obviously, he'd been a crafty devil and kept it to himself. Shortly after this the Mk Is were replaced.

'In the summer of 1943 there were strong rumours that the U-boats were being withdrawn to be fitted with much heavier anti-aircraft defences in order to fight it out on the surface. Rumour was of some magical gyroscopic gun mountings! Whatever the truth of

Above left: No 120 Squadron at Reykjavik, Iceland in July 1943. Front (left to right): Sgt Jeans; Plt Off Matthews; Flg Off Webber; Flt Sgt John Luker. Rear: Flg Off Barker; Sgt Allan; Flt Sgt Lea; and Sgt Bradley. /*J. Luker*

Left: Aerial view of the Liberator OTU at Nassau, in the Bahamas, in March 1944./*J. Luker*

Above: Liberator GR1, AM910, an early version in use by Coastal Command. Fitted with ASV radar aerials; also four 20mm cannon belly pack – though no nose gun turret. /*Author's Collection*

Right: Lib load. The motley mixture of depth charges, flame and smoke floats, sea markers, et al about to be put aboard a GR III Liberator on 26 February 1944./*IWM*

it my log book records a lot of anti-submarine sweeps in August 1943, between Iceland and the UK, Looking for U-boats returning to the Western Atlantic. One Hudson flying from Iceland did catch one on the surface and received such intensive gunfire that the action was broken off – eyebrows were raised! I mention this because in a TV programme on the Battle of the Atlantic (broadcast in January 1978) William Woollard said that at this time aircraft were *ordered* not to attack sighted U-boats but to home RN escorts to destroy the enemy. If this was an order, we never received it on our squadron. In any case it sounds ridiculous – no U-boat would remain surfaced if it suspected an aircraft was acting as a homing device.

'On 8 October 1943 – our first op after leave in the UK – we set off from Meeks Field on a convoy escort, flying Liberator III, "T" of No 120 Squadron (FK223). In daylight we flew either at 5,000ft or cloudbase (if lower). At 56° 18′N; 26° 30′W our radar operator (using the earlier limited-range ASV radar) reported a contact dead ahead at 10 miles. We the pilots, saw it almost simultaneously. "Action Stations!" Our skipper (Dennis Webber) pulled into cloud in the hope of making an undetected approach, but when we came out of it and roared in to attack we had insufficient time to get down to a proper height to drop our depth charges, so we did a

tight turn to make another run. I remember seeing lots of tracer whizzing underneath us and heavier flak bursting in black puffs above us – fortunately we weren't hit. We had one .50cal gun firing forward and four .303in Brownings in the rear turret, and all were used during the attacks.

'Second time round we arrived to attack from the bows because the armament of UBs was reported to be more deadly to the rear. However the UB easily out-turned us and our attack was more or less broadside on. We pressed home the attack in face of heavy fire and dropped one stick of four 250lb DCs from about 50ft. I don't know what the effect of this attack was – we didn't wait to find out but came in again to drop our second stick of four DCs from about 30ft; a perfect stick which entered the water and exploded as we banked away (wing span 110ft!) after the attack. As we passed over the U-boat on attack three I stuck my head into the blister in my side window and noted that guns and gunners seemed to have disappeared.

'The U-boat (U-643) stopped dead on the surface – we had no more DCs – and we were amazed to see all the crew tumble out on to the deck and conning tower wearing life-jackets and carrying dinghies. Another Lib [Liberator "Z" of No 86 Squadron, Flg Off Burcher. *Author*] joined us but we had thoughts of the homing destroyers catching a live U-boat and no more attacks were undertaken. Suspecting a ruse we kept a careful eye on the U-boat whilst awaiting arrival of the destroyers. Once the weather threatened to close in and we made low-level runs to drop smoke floats to mark its position. The U-boat crew thought we were attacking again and I saw their fists clenched and raised in anger. We replied suitably. Eventually the destroyers picked up the survivors but not before the crew had scuttled the U-boat. One minute it was there on the surface – the next it was gone without trace, except, of course, for the crew in their dinghies and life-jackets – they were lucky to survive.

'My log book suggests 15 survivors including the captain [Kapitänleutnant Speidel. *Author*] were rescued but we were not really sure of the number. We were also told later that photos showed the aerials of radar, not known previously to be carried by U-boats, though I cannot confirm this. Certainly the U-boat was ready for us when we came out of cloud – perhaps they simply heard us. Once the survivors had been rescued we had reached the PLE – Prudent Limit of Endurance – and turned for home. We never saw the convoy (SC143) we were to have escorted. Now we were diverted to Ballykelly because of bad weather at Reykjavik, and landed triumphantly after 15hr 50min. Dennis

Webber received an immediate award of the DFC, while the crew received a congratulatory telegram from the C-in-C Western Approaches sent to AOC Iceland.

'In November 1943 we were gradually re-equipped with Mk V Liberators, equipped with Leigh Lights and H2S radar, and converted to a night squadron for Leigh Light patrols. Conversion was done on the squadron to keep us operational and we were the first crew trained on 120. It was a dodgy business in winter, Icelandic weather, getting down to 50ft at night to home onto a moored buoy – we had no radar altimeters. We did our first op on 12 December – with heavier aircraft our flights were now about 12½hr endurance. In the early ops we had some odd experiences until the radar operators were sufficiently well practised at "reading" contacts. Once, in gathering dusk, we homed on to a contact only to see – just in time – the *Ile de France* looming up in front of us – no one had told us she would be in our patrol area. We homed on squalls and birds and God-knows-what but saw no more U-boats from Iceland. As a crew we flew our last (29th) op at the end of January 1944.

'I was now commissioned, due to have my own crew, so was asked would I like to collect a new crew from the Liberator OTU in Nassau? Had I converted on the squadron my maximum permitted 12 months in Iceland would have been up before I became operational. In the event the squadron itself returned to Ballykelly before I returned from Nassau with my new crew, and we rejoined 120 there in May 1944. The crew now numbered 10 but as we had not done any Leigh Light, training, which was not available in Nassau, we went to Aldergrove to convert the crew, flying Mk V and VI Libs. Back to the squadron for ops from Ballykelly, where we flew all anti-sub Leigh Light patrols – longest 15½hr – but saw no more U-boats. Once the UBs had Schnorkels we had few sightings, but at least they were kept away from the convoys of 1944. I flew my last operation on Christmas Day 1944 and then went "on rest" to Aldergrove, having completed 584 operational flying hours on Liberators – at which time we were converting to Mk VIII Libs. I stayed with 1674 HCU and 111(C) OTU at Aldergrove, Milltown and Lossiemouth until demob as a Flight Lieutenant, having by then logged 1,885hr as a pilot.'

Below: **On the job. Liberator GR VI, KG907, with under-radome extended over the the Atlantic, from Aldergrove.**/*W. V. Cluff*

Bottom: **On reflection. Liberator GR VI, KG904 of No 220 Squadron, in the Azores, April 1945, covered for weather protection. Nearby a Fordson tractor eases a twin-trolley load of depth charges through the Azores mud and rain. Note wing-mounted Leigh Light in upper foreground.**/*IWM*

Strike & Strike Again

For the first three years of Coastal Command's mammoth task of providing aerial umbrellas for Allied shipping across the Atlantic, operations were mainly concentrated on defeating the ubiquitous U-boats marauding along every shipping lane and convoy route. The ability to adopt any form of true offensive against Axis shipping was restricted in various ways; chiefly by the sheer lack of quantity of aircraft and crews available for other than anti-submarine sorties, but no less by the blatant lack of a suitable type of aircraft for direct anti-shipping strike operations. This latter function began to be resolved with the introduction of the Bristol Beaufort torpedo-bomber, yet these were too few in number, and of insufficiently high performance to undertake many of the more desirable forms of offensive against German mercantile shipping in long-range waters. Equally, the torpedo, though highly effective if used with skill and accuracy, was essentially a one-shot weapon – a distinctly hit-or-miss armament which left no room for an immediate repeat performance.

Temporary reinforcement of the Coastal anti-shipping offensive was undertaken from March to October 1941 by the Blenheim crews of 2 Group, Bomber Command. The unsurpassed courage of the Blenheim crews during those fateful months, despite horrifying casualty figures, was nevertheless only slightly rewarded by confirmed results. A total of 29 enemy vessels actually sunk, with a further 21 seriously damaged (as opposed to contemporary Air Ministry claims for some 170 vessels sunk or damaged). The 'fault', if there was one, was in the type of aircraft employed. The Blenheim IV day bomber was just not suitable for the task; a stark fact which also applied to Coastal's Hampden and other contemporary machines.

The answer to these problems came with the introduction of the Bristol Beaufighter in 1940; the first unit to receive the type being No 252 Squadron. The 'mighty Beau' offered a rare combination of high speed, rugged strength, endurance, multi-role adaptability, with a variety of choice in pure armament virtually unrivalled within the RAF. The Beaufighter eventually became operational within Coastal Command in early 1942 and made an immediate impact on the anti-shipping scene. Its potential was quickly stretched to take in every type of Coastal role; using its combined cannons, machine guns, rockets and bombs to cut a deadly swathe through any merchant convoys encountered. A further extension of the Beau's 'arm' was the modified variant able to carry a torpedo – the 'Torbeau' – though many individual crew members regarded this form of Beaufighter armament as a retrograde step. With typical vision of an even greater potential for the Beaufighter, the AOC-in-C, Coastal Command then, Philip Joubert, pressed Air Ministry to approve the formation of special Beaufighter 'strike Wings'; to combine three Beau units with differing operational roles in one formation, self-supported and mobile. Joubert's idea won acceptance, and in September 1942 a decision was taken to equip Coastal Command with 15 squadrons of Beaus by April 1943.

The first Strike Wing came into being in November 1942, at North Coates Fitties, comprised of three Beaufighter squadrons; Nos 143 (fighter-versions), 236 (fighter-bombers) and 254 (Torbeaus). The Wing's terms of reference were simple – to provide a formation of self-protected attack aircraft to tackle any shipping target of reasonable size around Britain's coastal waters within a Beaufighter's long range. Ostensibly fully trained and operationally fit, the Wing's first operation on 20 November – a heavily escorted enemy convoy steering south-west towards Rotterdam – was a near-disaster. Two Beau units, Nos 236 and 254 Squadrons, despatched their aircraft, but the subsequent claims for merely three ships damaged was offset by the loss of three Beaufighters, and a further four Beaus which crashed or force-landed on return. Clearly the tactical use of a strike Wing had yet to be fully appreciated; the Wing was immediately withdrawn for intensive training, and did not re-enter the lists until the following April.

Notwithstanding the semi-fiasco of Beaufighter Strike Wings' initial operations, by the summer of 1943 the Beau units began to justify Joubert's initiative superbly; ranging far and wide around Britain's coastline and exacting an ever-increasing toll of Germany shipping. Fighter Beaus were also prominent in the protective air escort role covering Coastal Command's anti-U-boat aircraft above the notorious Bay of Biscay, clashing on myriad occasions with the Luftwaffe's counterpart Junkers Ju88s and occasional Focke-Wulf Fw190s. In May 1943 the North Coates Wing received its first rocket-armed Beaus, and took the new weapon into action for the first time on 22 June 1943. The general tactic employed by then was to send in up to a dozen Torbeaus against any target first, covered and followed by up to 20 rocket or cannon-armed Beaus to 'finish the job'.

In early 1943 the Beaufighter was joined in Coastal Command by the de Havilland Mosquito – the 'Wooden Wonder' which was eventually to replace virtually all Beaufighters within the command by 1945. Apart from some PRU units, the first Mosquito-equipped

Coastal unit was No 333 (Norwegian) Squadron, which was formed from 1477 Flight at Leuchars on 10 May 1943. In Coastal Command the standard variant used was the Mk VI, but in October 1943 two Mosquito FB XVIIIs were first issued to No 248 Squadron, based at Predannack. These incorporated a 3.7in anti-aircraft cannon during initial works' trials and tests, and were eventually issued to the command with a 6lb Class M (Molins) 57mm gun. Only a dozen Mk XVIIIs were eventually produced, but these exemplified Coastal's insatiable search for effective anti-shipping weaponry throughout the war.

Both the Beaufighter and Mosquito squadrons were mainly intended for harassing surface shipping, rather than U-boats. In this role their depredations knew few bounds; ranging over the North Sea to Norway, along the northern European coastline, or south across the Irish Sea and the Biscay Bay. Anything

Below: **Early days. Blenheim IVs of No 235 Squadron set out for enemy waters, early 1941. Apart from usual guns, these had a four .303in Browning gun-pack under the belly, forward-firing, and controlled by the pilot.** */PNA Ltd*

Bottom: **Mighty Beau. The Bristol Beaufighter which first entered Coastal service with No 252 Squadron in 1940 – R2198, 'B-Baker' of that unit is illustrated – and quickly made an impact on the Command's strike capability and other offensive ops.** */IWM*

Above: Convoy clobber.
Beaufighters of the North
Coates Wing – No 143
Squadron here – batter a
German convoy on 22 June
1943./*Author's Collection*

Right: Low stuff.
Beaufighter's forward view
of a German flak ship as the
Beau completed its first
pass./*IWM*

bearing the crooked cross of Nazi Germany which floated was fair game to the ever-eager Strike Wing crews. By the closing months of the European war, with virtual complete air superiority in the hands of the Allied air services, the Coastal strike crews achieved an almost unparalled run of successes against the dwindling German surface (and underwater) fleets. Whether hiding in a remote Norwegian fiord, Danish harbour, French fishing port, or simply nestling among a host of heavily-gunned flak protector-vessels; no German ship was immune to attack. Sweeping in at deck-level, the strike crews shattered and smothered a host of enemy targets in a boiling holocaust of cannon and rocket fury; the death knell of any surviving Nazi hopes of continuing the war at sea.

The following first-hand accounts of typical strikes serve to some extent to illustrate the variety of types of operations flown by the Coastal strike crews. All are, perhaps characteristically, modest and under-stated in a long-standing RAF tradition of deliberate 'playing down' of any successes achieved. Yet each, in its own way, exemplifies the determination and courage needed to press home any attack, whatever the odds. Coastal

Above: Beaufighter NT961, PL-O, of No 144 Squadron at dispersal. This machine replaced the former PL-O, NE831, when the latter crashed on return from a sortie. /*C. B. Nicholl*

Left: Flt Lt M. C. 'Mike' Bateman, DFC, of No 236 Squadron, who sank the U-418 on 1 June 1943 with his Beaufighter's 3in RP armament – the first such sub-kill. /*IWM*

Above centre: Beau crew. Flg Off York (l) and his navigator Duncan Marrow, DFC, about to fly a sortie; No 144 Squadron, Dallachy, March 1945. /*D. Marrow*

Above right: Meanwhile, back in the locker room . . . Flg Off E. J. Keefe (l) and Sgt B. G. Steed – both Canadians – of No 404 Squadron, RCAF (Beaufighter at Tain, 29 July 1943. /*Public Archives of Canada*

Right: Mossie men. Crews of No 143 Squadron at Manston, 1944. At least one-third of these men were later killed in action. /*N. Carr*

Command's official motto, 'Constant Endeavour,' was particularly apt when applied to the men of the command's Beaufighter and Mosquito crews.

Among the first Beaufighter pilots to use the 3in rocket on Coastal operations was Wg Cdr R. H. McConnell, DFC (later DSO), of No 235 Squadron. His account of his first rocket strike recalled the excitement (sic) of his crew at the prospect, and an intensive training period in use of RP. Hugh McConnell continues:

'Our first attack followed a report by a Norwegian Mosquito pilot of a medium-sized merchant vessel which had become stranded in a Norwegian fiord just east of North Christiansaand, not far from Trondheim. We stood by all day hoping to be led to the target by a Mosquito, but the weather closed in and we had to wait patiently for it to clear. Owing to the difficulty of keeping formation in bad weather, and trying to keep up with a much faster Mosquito, it was decided that the Mosquito pilot should stand behind me in my leading Beaufighter and direct us to the enemy ship. On the Sunday six of our Beaufighters took off at six o'clock in the evening. Three from my squadron were to shoot up the ship

Left: **Mosquito bite. Mosquito F of No 143 Squadron 'on target' against shipping at Leirvik, Norway, on 15 January 1945.** */ACM Sir C. Foxley-Norris*

Below: **Wg Cdr R. H. McConnell, DSO, DFC, of No 235 Squadron.** */IWM*

Above: Mosquito RP attack on shipping in Edj Fiord, on 25 January 1945, by Flg Off Norman Carr in 'Q-Queenie' of No 143 Squadron/.*N. Carr*

Left: Cutting it close. Beaufighters smother a vessel close to the shore-line of a Norwegian fiord on 5 May 1945. On original print five Beaufighters are visible here, apart from the sixth which took the shot; close company at high speed between towering cliff-faces. /*IWM*

Above right: Ready to go. Fully armed Beaufighters of No 236 Squadron stand by, October 1944. Each carries a battery of eight 3in RP under the wings, with 25lb Semi-Armour Piercing (SAP) rocket heads for the anti-shipping role. Electrical leads ('Pigtails') remain unplugged until the aircraft actually starts up – a safety measure./*Author's Collection*

Right: Torbeau. Torpedo Beaufighter pictured on 15 May 1943./*IWM*

with RP, while the other three were to act as fighter escort. The crews were warned that they had to be careful when approaching the target owing to the steep hills surrounding the fiords. We had to approach over the hills, coming in low, firing quickly and passing out over the heavily defended harbour entrance.

'The weather was bad at the start, but after 15 minutes' flying we came out into a cloudless sky and unlimited visibility. I led the formation very low up the Norwegian coast. Three small escort ships signalled us with an Aldis lamp and we flashed back a reply. They took us for Hun aircraft. Then we flew low over the inhabited islands and could see the islanders in their Sunday clothes taking an evening stroll. We came to a field where some Germans were playing football and they ran for their lives.

'It was 1930 when we climbed over the hills to make our attack. The enemy had been firing at us for some time but had not come near us. There was also a hail of fire from the shore ack-ack. batteries. When we had flown over the hill we had to be quick on the trigger or we would have passed over the enemy ship. In fact, I didn't have sufficient time to fire at first, nor did my No 2 Beaufighter, but No 3 spotted the ship a little sooner and opened fire with his RP. I turned round up the fiord and made a second attack, this time scoring hits on the ship; No 2 following me scored several more. Meanwhile the Beaufighters of

the other squadron were circling as protection against enemy fighters. I saw the ship catch fire at the stern and she was burning brightly when two Messerschmitt Bf109s appeared and attacked No 3 Beaufighter. At the time the Beau's observer was busy holding a camera over the side, taking photographs, and he first he knew that enemy fighters were bout was when a bullet hit his camera.

'We flew out to sea and managed to shake off the fighters, but No 3 Beau was badly shot up, with the undercarriage out of action and a hole in one of its petrol tanks. One of our escorting Beaus, which was also attacked, turned away from the coast and was subsequently missing. We regained base and No 3 Beau made a successful belly-landing on a small runway; its observer was slightly wounded.'

In a galaxy of prominent Beaufighter strike-leaders, one of the most outstanding was undoubtedly Wg Cdr A. K. Gatward, DSO, DFC (later Air Cdr RAF (Rtd). Gatward first came into the glare of press publicity when, on 12 June 1942 flying Beaufighter T4800, ND-C of No 236 Squadron, he flew alone to German-occupied Paris. On arrival he had dropped a French tricolour over the Arc d'Triomphe, and then rounded out his sortie by cannon-blasting the local Gestapo headquarters' building. On 1 April 1944, Gatward succeeded to the command of No 404 (Buffalo) squadron, RCAF, the first Canadian unit under the aegis of RAF Coastal Command. On 8 August 'Ken' Gatward led a formation of 15 Beaus of No 404

Squadron, and nine more from No 236 Squadron, in a strike against a reported gaggle of enemy ships between Belle Ile and the French mainland. Taking off at 1620, Gatward led his men straight out to sea towards the indicated area, but on arrival found nothing to attack. In Gatward's words:

'We saw a few old fishermen who waved to us, and there were children in some of the fishing boats, who waved too.

'We flew south and, just as we approached the extreme end of Bourgeneuf Bay, I spotted four German minesweepers, all stationary and bunched together, on a calm sea. We wheeled to port and I gave the old cry of *Attack, Attack!*; ordering the port section to take the port ship, and the starboard section to take the starboard ships, leaving the middle one to me. Flak came up from the shore, 1,000yd away, and the minesweepers opened fire at two miles' range. They kept it up until we opened with our cannon at 1,000yd, after which the fire from the ships died down. However, it continued to come fairly thick from the shore, near Fromentine. One of our Beaufighters bought it; R. S. Forestall was

the pilot and I. C. Robbie his navigator, both Canadians. I had seen their tracer coming in with mine, so they must have been shot down during the attack, just before their aircraft crashed close to the ships.

'As we closed range to about 400yd we fired off our rockets. Soon three of the ships were on fire and the fourth was smoking. There were great clouds of smoke – very satisfactory. It was always miserable to look back after any attack and see ships unharmed on the water. We went over the tops of the ships and broke out to sea. Then the pilot of one Beau called up to say that he had "lost" an engine, and if I'd escort him home. At that moment a second Beau pilot called up to say "It's all right, I'm with him", and a third signalled "I'm with you". As I had the rest of the formation with me, and saw that the crippled aircraft was escorted on either side, I went on.

'Then one of our naval vessels called us up, saying that they understood from our chatter that we had some luck. I signalled back, "We think it's too small for you to bother about", but they answered, "Nothing is too small for us!" So I answered, "Right, go ahead, and

Right: Big fist. Mosquito FB XVIII – the so-called 'Tsetse' – displays its nose armament of one 57mm cannon, plus four .303in Browning machine guns. The corporal gives scale to the size of just one 57mm shell./*Author's Collection*

Below: Tsetse. Mosquito FB XVIII, PZ468, QM-D of No 254 Squadron at North Coates, June 1945. This aircraft had seen previous service with No 248 Squadron. /*Ministry of Aircraft Production, Crown copyright*

good luck". So we left the three minesweepers in flames, and toddled home along the coast, seeing nothing on the way but a few fishing boats.'

Although the main task for the Beaufighter and Mosquito squadrons was to harass and attack all enemy shipping, part of their duty included air protection of Allied convoys and other merchant or Royal Navy vessels. The latter duty was never an easy one. Too often the crews were despatched at minimal notice, allowing little time for pre-planning on weather conditions, enemy opposition to be met, or even any precise location of the vessels they were expected to protect. Once arrived over their designated charges, the reception from their ostensibly friendly naval comrades-in-arms was often distinctly unfriendly – throughout the air-sea war naval anti-aircraft gunners gained a certain notoriety for their trigger-happy greeting to all and sundry aircraft within shooting range; a graphic adherence to the old cliche, 'Shoot first, ask questions later'. All of which was accepted by Coastal's strike crews as merely part of the job, and they remained ever-ready to help their 'web-footed' brethren if at all possible.

These protection duties often gave the Beaufighters and Mosquitos a pure fighting role, tackling Luftwaffe aircraft attempting to copy the strike role. This was the case on 21 July 1944 when two Mosquitos of No 235 Squadron were ordered to fly an air umbrella patrol above a naval destroyer escort group off Ushant. Weather conditions were foul, but the two Mosquito crews set out, having received a report that the destroyers were being harassed by several Dorniers, carrying glider bombs. Boring their way through dense clouds and mist down to sea level, through continuous driving rain, the two aircraft deliberately separated to avoid any possible air collision, but as they did so one Mosquito dipped a wing into the sea and crashed at high speed. The second Mosquito eventually returned to base, to report that weather conditions were nigh impossible to penetrate.

Wg Cdr J. V. Yonge, highly conscious of the need to provide air cover for the destroyer group, decided to fly the sortie himself, in company with one volunteer crew (Flg Off Frost/Flg Off Fuller). Yonge, 38 years old and first commissioned in the RAF in December 1925, was a veteran flier who knew the risks involved; but undertook the sortie calmly, without any false heroics as motivation – it was 'his job':

'When Frost and I took off the weather had cleared a little over base, but we had to fly blind, in close formation, to get through the rain and low cloud. We finally broke cloud at 1,400ft while approaching the patrol area. Then we came into a patch of weather the like of which I had never seen before. We were in a col, with a thunderstorm to the south, sea fog over Brest and Ushant, and continuous rain to the north; it was the most extraordinary combination of weather. Then we reached the patrol area and it was comparatively clear, but we had to vary our height and fly blind from time to time to keep at our task.

'At 20 minutes past one I had still not found either the destroyers or the reported Dorniers. Then, half an hour later, we sighted two Dornier Do217s, with a Mosquito from another Wing opening fire on them at long range. I learned later that the Mosquito was an ADGB

Below: **Brock's Benefit. On 21 April 1945 a formation of Mosquitos returning from a strike in the Kattegat, intercepted 18 German torpedo-bombers, and destroyed nine of these within minutes. This view from one Mosquito shows a Luftwaffe machine exploding as it hit the sea.** /*British Official*

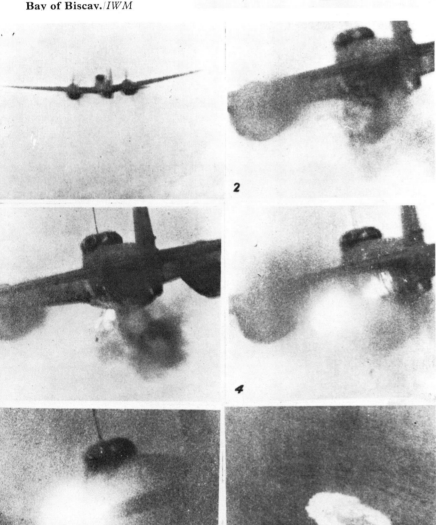

aircraft, and that it was still trying to attack after being hit in its port engine. The pilot had to give it up and fly home as best he could. We jettisoned our wing tanks, opened up to full boost and revs, and attacked the second Dornier at 300kts. I was just about to open fire when I saw that Frost had already set its port engine on fire. I therefore swung my gunsight on to the leading Dornier and attacked with several bursts of cannon and .303in, opening at 800yd. I closed right behind its tail, although he was doing his best to dodge me. Out of the corner of my eye I saw the first German, which Frost had hit, diving in flames and three parachutes floating down to the water.

'My fire was effective. The Dornier blew up, 100yd in front of me, so close that streams of his oil blacked me out completely. I had to jerk back the stick to avoid hitting him, and then to fly on instruments until the windscreen wiper had cleaned some of the oil away. Then I could just about peer through the relatively clear spots between the thick German oil and saw the two Dorniers blazing on the sea, and several of the crews in dinghies.

'It was only then that we saw the destroyers we were defending from the Dorniers for the first time. I spoke to the Navy and told them that both Germans had been shot down in flames, and that the survivors were waiting in the water to be picked up. Frost and I became separated in the thick cloud on the way back, but we landed at base within five minutes of each other. Here I handed the Mosquito over to the ground crew, always there to make us feel that they were part of the effort. They wiped the thick oil from the fuselage; then painted a swastika on it for our victory.'

97

Reap the
Whirlwind

Left: U-625 about to be sunk on 10 March 1944 by depth charges from Sunderland EK591/'U' of No 422 Squadron RCAF. /*Public Archives of Canada*

Below left: Pass-over. Beaufighters crossing over their targets on 24 July 1944. /*IWM*

Right: Rockets from Mosquito 'D' of No 143 Squadron find their mark at Porsgrunn on 11 April 1945./*ACM Sir C. Foxley-Norris*

Below: The Coastal Command strike offensive was pursued until the very end; exemplified here by a Mosquito ('T' of No 143 Squadron) attack on an enemy convoy on 4 May 1945 – only days before the European cease-fire. /*ACM Sir C. Foxley-Norris*

Above left: Sub-strike. On 9 April 1945 a Mosquito Wing sank three submarines by direct RP and cannon attacks – U-804, U-843 and U-1065. In this camera shot from Mosquito 'Z' of No 143 Squadron, two of the submarines are being attacked simultaneously. /ACM Sir C. Foxley-Norris

Left: No safe harbour. German merchant vessel moored at Tetgenaes on 23 March 1945 is discovered by Mosquito 'G' of No 143 Squadron. /ACM Sir C. Foxley-Norris

Above: Blohm und Voss Ha138 flying boat makes its last sortie. One victim of No 404 Squadron, RCAF's Beaufighters on 28 August 1943, off the coast of Scotland. /IWM

Right: Death plunge. U-426 sinking by the stern on 8 January 1944 after a depth charge assault by Sunderland 'U-Uncle' of No 10 Squadron, RAAF, piloted by Flg Off J. P. Roberts. /IWM

Above: Surrender – 1. *Nurnberg*, a 6,000-ton cruiser, making its last voyage, off the Danish coast on 20 May 1945, escorted by Coastal Liberators. /*D. V. Quinn*

Right: Surrender – 2. U-516, displaying the mandatory black flag, surrenders to Sunderland skipper Flt Lt Allardice, No 461 Squadron, RAAF./*Author's Collection*

Below right: Surrender – 3. A Schnorchel-equipped U-boat surfaces at Londonderry, May 1945. /*Author's Collection*

Far right, top: Surrender – 4. U-244, viewed from a Liberator on 13 May 1945 (150ft height) at position 56.06N/13.34W; blowing tanks and displaying the black surrender 'flag'. /*Author's Collection*

Far right, bottom: Surrender – 5. U-363 in peaceful waters. Note extra flak platforms forward of conning tower./*L. Worner*

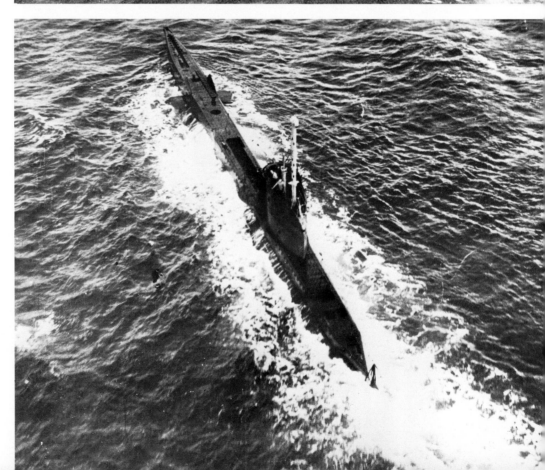

Above: Surrender – 6. The unique occasion when U-570 'surrendered' to Lockheed Hudson 'S' of No 269 Squadron on 27 August 1941. The Hudson skipper, Sqn Ldr J. H. Thompson, was awarded a DFC for his feat; while the submarine was later re-used by the Royal Navy as HMS *Graph*. /D. Lyall

Right: Surrender – 7. U-825, viewed from 100ft, making 14kts, at the point 54.55N/11.36W on 11 May 1945./Author's Collection

Below right: Surrender – 8. U-643 surfaces and surrenders to Liberator 'T-Tommy' FK223, of No 120 Squadron on 8 October 1943 at position 56.18N/26.30W. It had been successfully attacked by Liberators 'Z' of No 86 Squadron (Flg Off C. W. Burcher) and 'T' of No 120 Squadron (Flg Off D. Webber), but was then scuttled by its captain. /J. Luker

Ditched

Mathematicians tell us that some two-thirds of the globe is covered by oceans. Doubtless they could also calculate the theoretical chances of spotting, from the sky, a minute rubber dinghy and its occupants; drifting helplessly on the currents of a vista of blue-grey-green sea waters which have no apparent parameters. Whatever that figure may be, it must be virtually infinitesimal. To the crews of Coastal Command engaged in the unending struggle across the Atlantic such awesome odds against survival in the event of ditching far from land were a permanent corollary to their 'routine' tasks; dreaded perhaps but accepted as merely part of the job. The sea seldom gives up its secrets, thus we shall never know precisely the circumstances in which so many Coastal crews simply 'failed to return'. Too often the last contact with such crews was a faint, distorted R/T signal, advising base that the crew was about to attack a U-boat, or had some mechanical failure necessitating landing – or rather, attempting to land – on the open ocean. Then – silence.

Yet – astonishingly – many crews did survive such a ditching. The physical and psychological ordeal many of such crews underwent before eventual retrieval can only be described as horrific. That such men overcame theoretically impossible odds and still lived can only serve as tribute to man's inherent will to survive, and individual stubborn determination and uncommon courage. In a majority of known cases the aircraft was forced to ditch due to damage inflicted by U-boat flak guns, leaving the aircraft skipper to use every ounce of his skill in accomplishing some sort of landing in a machine which was barely, if at all, controllable. The moment of impact with the ocean – likened to 'hitting a concrete wall at 200mph in a tin barrel' by one surviving skipper – almost invariably broke up the aircraft; causing further injuries to crew members, apart from shock and concussion. With (usually) only a matter of seconds before a wrecked aircraft slid beneath the waves, each man had to act swiftly, whatever his physical condition. Then came the frantic search for a dinghy or something solid to cling to for support in the heaving water. If they were

lucky, the surviving crew could scramble into a dinghy and set about their daunting task of clinging to life. All had received survival training, but theory in the comfortable surrounds of a classroom or local swimming pool bore little relation to the stark reality of crashing into the sea and facing raw nature day and night, often for days on end.

Few men, relatively, posted to Coastal Command had any previous close experience of the sea, beyond occasional pottering about in coastal waters in tiny vessels or in fresh-water rivers. Indeed, an ability to swim was not even considered an essential pre-requisite to any such posting. Thus, the men of a ditched crew more often than not were totally ignorant of the sheer power of uncontrollable elements inherent in vast oceans. Searing sun by day, freezing gales, howling surface winds, constant soaking by salt water, ever-present danger of capsizing in heaving, gigantic roller waves of any ocean swell – all quickly reduced a human being to a perilous state. Sea, sun and winds, allied to crippling see-saws of extreme temperatures combined to make an implacable foe; more Coastal Command crews were killed by nature than by any designated 'enemy'.

The one constant ray of hope afforded to any ditched crew was the certain knowledge that, once reported 'missing' from any patrol, they would become immediately the focal point of a vast effort by their comrades back home to rescue them if humanly possible. A common hazard binds any esoteric community into a close-bound, near-family relationship, and the men of Coastal Command were famed for their close-knit feeling of comradeship – a bond which had originated with the pre-1939 RAF 'Flying boat union' of all airmen who served in, first, RAF Coastal Area and then Coastal Command. No effort was ever spared to retrieve a lost crew – as long as there was even the slimmest chance of rescuing a ditched crew, other crews undertook long and often hazardous attempts to 'bring 'em back alive'. The motto of the in-shore Air Sea Rescue Service was 'The sea shall not have them', and men of the Coastal squadrons exemplified that spirit on every possible occasion.

Those men who eventually survived the ordeal of a lengthy ditching in the sea seldom forgot it for the rest of their lives; the experience became an indelible memory. Yet only in rare exceptional cases did such an experience deter them from continuing on operational duties. In a few cases, survivors managed to make a form of daily diary of their experience – in itself a tribute to their calm determination to live. Such first-hand accounts, however brief, give inklings of the sufferings and problems of being 'cast upon the waters'. One such diarist was Grp Capt Roger Mead, DFC, AFC [later Air Cdre R. Mead, CBE, DFC, AFC, RAF, Rt'd]. His Halifax was hit by flak during an attack on a U-boat and set on fire, leaving him no alternative but to ditch. Of his crew only six men survived the crash, and Mead's notes give a vivid description of their 11-day nightmare.

'*First day:* Decided to eat and drink nothing for two days, All badly shocked. I was knocked about a bit. First wireless operator/air gunner burned on face. All seasick. But none seriously hurt and all in pretty good condition. First night cold and wet.

'*Second day:* Drizzle. Crew's condition excellent. All chirped up a lot and kept our heads, convinced we would be picked up.

'*Third day:* Drizzle at first, but we dried our clothes when weather cleared up. Tried some fishing. Made lines out of some odd earth and aerial wires and fish-hooks with safety pins. No luck. Found some chocolate spoiled by water; ate half an ounce and two milk tablets each. Bad night – cold, wet, and very uncomfortable. Between us kept watch all night, guessing the hours. Those nights were hell.

'*Fourth day:* Issued one small piece of chewing gum apiece; given back at lunchtime for bait. Again no fish. Two milk tablets each. Said morning and evening prayers. Another bad night – cold and wet. Water slopping over into dinghy.

'*Fifth day:* Nice, fine day. Clothes dry. Decided on one milk tablet each, four times a day. Had my shoes and socks off when sea rose to real Atlantic swell and overturned us. Kept our emergency rations but lost a lot of clothes. Difficult now to keep warm, especially feet, but all lucky to get back into dinghy. Thoroughly done in and badly shocked after that – Special issue of barley sugar – one each. Bucked us up. Sea rough all night; all wet and miserable. Dinghy water-logged all the time. Kept baling out.

'*Sixth day:* Poor weather, drizzle. Caught rain-water in our hands and drank it. Weather improved in afternoon. Sun-bathed, dried our clothes and Mae Wests. Dinghy doing extremely well. Ration still four milk tablets a day. In the evening opened first tin of water, shared round carefully. Determined to have a comfortable night, but very cold and all stiff and miserable. At 0200 saw a light on the horizon. Fired a signal, then found it was only Mars.

Below: Dinghy, Dinghy. Survivors of U-243 in the Bay of Biscay on 8 July 1944, after the submarine had been sunk by Flg Off W. B. Tilley, RAAF, in Sunderland 'H' of No 10 Squadron, RAAF. They were later retrieved by an Allied destroyer called to the spot by Tilley./*IWM*

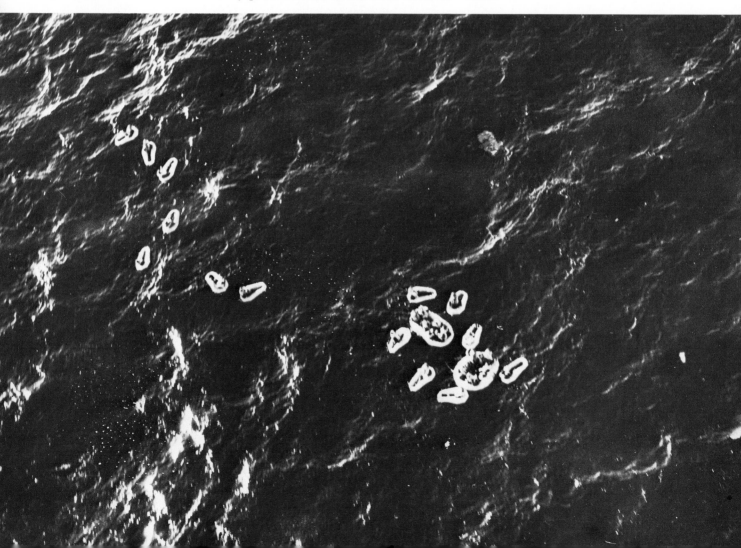

'*Seventh day:* Warm. Dried everything out and bathed in the afternoon, one after the other. Frightened by a couple of whales basking and bellowing 400yd away. All wounds healing well. Had a discussion on what action to take. Decided to reach patrol area of the Bay (of Biscay). Still trying hard to catch fish. Made fishing net from half a mast and a seat of old pair of pants. No fish, but at about 1800 caught an unlimited number of jelly fish, all sizes, and what looked like baby octopi. Tried to make a drink out of them. Foul. Seemed to be mainly water. Dubious stuff altogether. Kept it in case we got thirsty. Night warm and dry. Sea calm.

'*Eighth day:* Low cloud, turning to warm sun. Made and shipped a two-sheet sail. Most effective. Crew now breathing through sea-wetted handkerchiefs and keeping hair and faces wet to reduce evaporation losses. Hope still high but night bad. All getting tired easily. Most of the crew lying all the time on the floor. Sea rough but maintained a good speed all night.

'*Ninth day:* Very rough. Great strain on all. Shipped water continuously. Night an absolute nightmare. Very rough, raining hard. Afraid of being tipped in the water at any moment. Everything soaked.

'*Tenth day:* Crew very tired. Special issue of chocolate – two small cubes each. Weather improved in the afternoon after three distinct storms. Using pocket compass; hope to reach patrol area in two days. Night: no notes.

'*Eleventh day:* Weather cleared mid-day. Divided one tin of water among us – two ounces each. A little chocolate.'

At that stage Roger Mead became '. . . too dopey' either to write or even read his notes. One of the crew in the dinghy, Flt Sgt G. R. E. Robertson, later added to Mead's brief descriptions; recalling his own increasingly confused reactions to their situation. He told of the many hours spent fruitlessly fishing over the side of the dinghy, using pieces of their wound scabs and the soft skin between their toes as bait. Hunger, thirst and decreasing physical condition played on his mind, until he reached a euphoric calm state of mind in which he considered – quite calmly – whether it would be best to die slowly of thirst, slide over the side and drown quickly, or drink the salt sea water and go mad. His heightened imagination saw big fish in the sea below the dinghy '. . . like dolphins, staring from the depths . . .' At 1430 on the 11th day Mead's crew spotted the mast of a destroyer, then, dazedly, realised that a second destroyer was on their other side. Too weak to help themselves, the crew was taken aboard. They were later told that the destroyers had discovered the dinghy by pure chance – they were not actually looking for it.

Mead's crew's ordeal makes grim enough reading, yet – and it is merely relative in the broadest sense – they were fortunate in certain facets of their initial situation. Though all had

Below: **A friend in need. Stranded Saro London of No 202 Squadron accepting a tow from the Royal Navy, August 1940. Though not identified positively, this was almost certainly K5909, being rescued by the destroyer HMS *Forester*; though it may have been another No 202 Squadron London, K5260, which ditched on 12 August but sank under tow.** /*Author's Collection*

been injured and shocked in some degree, they were mainly physically fit at the outset, with no serious effects from their crash-landing in the sea. In many cases, however, those who survived the crash were so badly injured, or suffering already from wounds inflicted by a U-boat's flak guns, that the additional imposition of days in an open dinghy, at the mercy of the elements, was more than even the stoutest body could endure. Their deaths in the dinghy added deep anguish to the already parlous condition of their fellow crew survivors. Flight Sergeant Jack Foss, second pilot in a Liberator forced to ditch after an air combat over the notorious Bay of Biscay, was another survivor who kept brief notes on his experience. Only seven of the original crew got out of the sinking Liberator – all of them wounded and injured in varying degrees – leaving two gunners behind who simply 'disappeared'. Interrogated afterwards in his hospital bed, Foss gave this account:

'After we had been shot down, those who were left – only seven of us – climbed into a dinghy. A gunner had died during the ditching and another had disappeared into the sea. For supplies we had only two small tins of orange juice, three emergency food boxes, two emergency rations, one lemon – but no flares or signalling apparatus. The first evening we noticed smoke on the horizon. We waved the telescopic flag and a vessel ap-

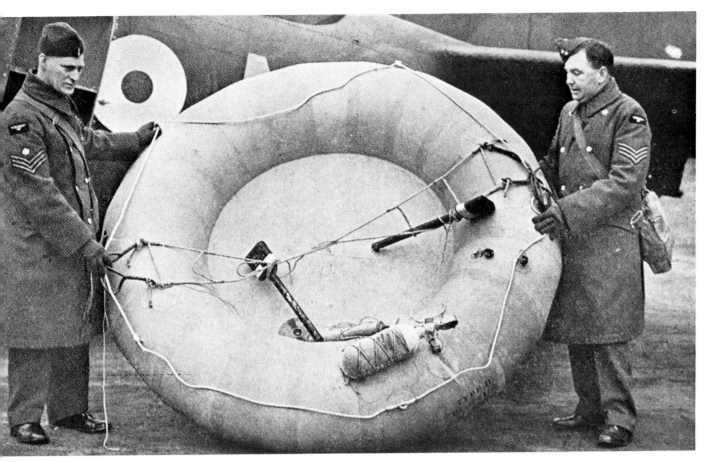

Above left: **Beaufort crew about to be rescued by a collier off the west Scottish coast, 1941.**/*Author's Collection*

Left: **Friend or foe. Four bedraggled U-boat crew survivors coming alongside an Allied vessel, 1943.** /*Author's Collection*

Above: **An early type of air crew dinghy, with air bottle, paddles-cum-distress signal holders (two), and little else.** /*Author's Collection*

proached. It was a U-boat and the crew lined up on deck wearing full uniform. An officer called out, *"Allierten oder nicht Allierten?"* (Allies or not?). One of us shouted, "English". Another said, "Water". The U-boat waited no more and made off – not one of the enemy crew said another word to us; and we didn't dare say another word as we were afraid they would turn their guns on us.' Foss's notes continue his story:

'*Second day:* Sighted Sunderland (flying boat). Tried to signal but failed. Sea moderated slightly. Flying Officer .... in agony with wounds. Flying Officer .... tried to keep him warm.

'*Third day:* 1800. An aircraft sighted in distance. Sea became rough. Crew saturated. Drifting fast.

'*Fourth day:* Liberator and Sunderland sighted but too far away.

'*Fifth day:* Sighted by Sunderland which circled dropping tins of water and emergency rations, which crew salvaged. Also first-aid kit but salt water rendered this u/s. Flares and sea-markers dropped. At night two Catalinas seen but they did not see us.

'*Sixth day:* Crew very hopeful but nothing sighted apart from distant Sunderland. Flying Officer .... died just before midnight and was buried at sea. Gangrene had set in on his wounds.

'*Seventh day:* Early morning a Sunderland arrived, followed by another Sunderland.

Supplies were dropped including medical kit, which the crew were too weak to haul aboard but recovered the parachute, dried it, and used as protection against breaking waves. Flying Officer .... died and was buried at sea.

'*Eighth day:* Early morning Catalina circled dropping flares. Crew answered with distress cartridges previously dropped them. One flare fell back into dinghy and was thrown out. Sergeant ...., wounded between shoulder blades, became very weak. Second Catalina arrived, then left to direct naval sloop to dinghy. Crew picked up at 0945.'

A tragic footnote to Jack Foss's diary was to record that his navigator and the flight engineer both died aboard the sloop, finally succumbing to their untreated wounds and the prolonged exposure.

The general tactic of remaining surfaced to fight it out with any attacking aircraft by U-boat crews during mid-1943 may seem to have been foolhardy to any layman. Yet the odds against the aircraft were greater than is often supposed. Any aircraft on its attack run was forced to fly at very low level and – most significantly – commence that run from a reasonable range, maintaining a rock-steady flight into the target U-boat. Thus the multiple cannon and machine gun crews on the submarine's conning tower were presented with an unwavering sitting duck at which to

Above: **Wg Cdr R. B. Thompson, DSO, commander of No 206 Squadron in June 1943. Later retired as AVM, CB, DSO, DFC.**/*IWM*

fire. It required cool nerves and utter determination for any pilot to deliberately nose his aircraft into the teeth of such flak opposition; qualities which were never lacking in any Coastal Command skipper. The cost of such courage was often high, and many aircraft were lost to U-boat guns in these air-sea gun battles.

Wg Cdr R. B. Thomson, DSO, commander of 206 Squadron at Benbecula, set out on 11 June 1943 in Fortress FA704 'R' on an anti-submarine patrol, and several hours later, from an altitude of 1,500ft, spotted a surfaced submarine some seven miles ahead. Thomson reported later:

'When I saw the U-boat dead ahead, I went straight for her, ordering all guns manned and the bomb doors opened. I came down to sea level and held steadily towards her. The U-boat opened fire at 400yd and I could feel her stuff hitting us, but carried on over her at about 50ft, dropping the depth charges and turning off as soon as the conning tower was below. As I turned the U-boat was at right-angles to its original track, but forging through the depth charge scum, and I thought to myself that I'd missed. Suddenly things started to happen. The plumes rose high as a flash of light seemed to ripple over the surface, and then the bows rose straight up – it was the reverse of a crash-dive. The U-boat started to sink back and I yelled at the top of my voice through the intercomm, "For Heaven's sake, take photos!" Within one

minute of the attack the U-boat had entirely disappeared – that was one U-boat which was certainly killed. [U-417: *Author.*]

'I flew over the spot and saw 20 to 30 Germans lying in the water looking up at us, and I was just saying "Poor blighters, they've had it" – as it was pretty cold that far north and there wasn't a ship within miles that could pick them up – when my second pilot broke in and shook me stiff, saying, "Don't look now, skipper, but oil and petrol are coming out of No 3 engine." I did look and saw that the engine appeared to be falling out of its mountings. I didn't get time to worry about it, as No 1 and No 2 engines then started shaking and refused to answer my controls. Only No 4 engine responded – it was clear I'd have to ditch. All this happened within about five minutes and the sight of the U-boat crew in the water, some of them shaking their fists at us, was still clear in my mind as I put her down. Thank the Lord it was a sweet landing and nobody was seriously injured. We all clambered into the only dinghy that would inflate, but unfortunately the store-packs came adrift so we had no food, water, distress signals or paddles.'

During its run-in to attack Thomson's Fortress had been hit in the nose, wings, bomb bay, cockpit and rear turret, apart from three of its four engines; though none of the crew had been wounded by some stroke of sheer luck. Once ditched, Thomson had dived into the sea to recover the only inflatable dinghy to be seen, but the rough seas meant that he could only hold on to it while the rest of his crew swam over to clamber into it. Just before ditching, however, an R/T SOS had been sent to base, where the rescue operation immediately swung into action.

At about 1900 that day the first would-be rescuer – a USN Catalina from Iceland – circled the dinghy and then attempted to land for a pick-up. As one of the ditched crew said later:

'The chances were all against him. We saw him circling and thought he was "fixing" us for other aircraft or ships. Then we saw his wing floats go down and realised he was going to try a landing. All our hopes went out to him for his as well as our sakes. His first touchdown was near-perfect but a big wave hit the Cat, the starboard prop flew off, and she buried her nose straight into the sea. We watched the crew taking to two dinghies, and within half an hour the Catalina had disappeared.'

For the next 24 hours both ditched crews remained in sight of each other, but could not link up due to the heavy seas. As one of Thomson's gunners, Flg Off J. L. Humphreys, described the conditions:

'It was heart-breaking. We had no paddles and they couldn't reach us. We could only wave at each other. Then in the evening the wind freshened to about 45kts and we knew we were in for a rough night. Seas rose to about 45ft high and, although we hauled the cover over our dinghy and clipped it down, plenty of water got in and we had to bale hard all night, using a pair of shoes. It was bitterly cold.'

During the second day a Catalina and a Fortress appeared and dropped supply boxes but these fell too far from Thomson's crew to be retrieved. When the next day dawned the American crew had vanished. They were, in fact, rescued many miles away but there was only one American survivor. Thomson's account continues:

'On the third day, in the afternoon, another Fortress found us and accurately dropped two supply packs. We got them both, and these contained water, corned beef, milk tablets and other necessities. It was the first food we'd had in 50 hours – up to then we'd been too seasick to bother with the thought of food. Half an hour later a Catalina arrived and dropped two more containers, comprising more food, plus cigarettes, matches, medical kit and some very welcome chemical hot-water bottles. Our armament officer who had come along "for the ride" was grey with cold – after our rescue he went down with pneumonia. In mid-afternoon we had another

visitor – a Sunderland from a Norwegian squadron – which made two valiant attempts to land. It was heroic, and each time the flying boat came in it hit heavy seas and was thrown 20ft into the air. We hid our eyes, thinking it must crash. The Sunderland's captain, however, realised that he hadn't a hope in such a heavy swell and, thank God, abandoned the attempt.'

Unknown to Thomson's crew they had ditched in the middle of a mined area, and though High Speed Launches (HSLs) of the Air Sea Rescue Service were already speeding to the spot, the mines would obviously prevent speedy rescue. Back in Group Head-quarters Sqn Ldr J. A. Holmes, DFC, of No 190 Squadron, a veteran Coastal skipper, volunteered to fly a Catalina for a pick-up attempt. With a crew of five, and his aircraft (FP102 'L') stripped of all unnecessary gear, Holmes took off:

'We set course very carefully, and had a minimum petrol load in order not to lose time. After about three hours we located the dinghy – a tiny yellow dot on a vast grey sea. Flying low to size up the state of the sea and the best position for landing, I ordered my crew to prepare our own dinghies in case we crashed, then turned in to land. Throttling back I came in slow with the nose high, cleared one big lump of sea by a touch of engines, then stalled onto the water. The Catalina bounced twice, hovered, then fell back onto the water with an

Above: **Pick-up. Though never intended for open-ocean landings, the Sunderland featured in many individual daring attempts to retrieve ditched fellow crews; as witnessed here on 22 September 1944.** */IWM*

impact which shook the whole aircraft. Luckily there was no damage, and I then caught sight of the dinghy.

'We taxied towards it, crabwise, and it was a slow job because every time I tried to turn the aircraft dug its nose in and we took green over the bows. At last we managed to throw the Fortress crew a line, and when we hauled the dinghy in it seemed incredible that eight people could be crowded into so small a space. They looked weary and bedraggled and hung on to our line for dear life; yet they managed a grin and a word of thanks as they came aboard. We took the weakest of them on the bunks and the others sat on the fuselage floor as we made ready for take-off. None of us were quite sure just what might happen in the next 60sec – there were 13 of us aboard. We shouted to the passengers to brace themselves and to expect some bounces before we became airborne. A clear lane opened up in the seas ahead, so I pushed the throttles fully open and we surged forward. I'd decided to haul back everything at 50kts, relying upon power to hold us in the air. We rushed over one swell, down into the trough, then up the side of another. Then we were thrown into the air as the needle touched fifty. There we stayed – she came off like a bird.'

Faith in the capabilities of the rescue services was an all-important psychological factor for ditched crews. To be able to rely on the knowledge that no effort would be spared to retrieve them from the ocean was vital as a mental boost to the normal human survival instinct. By 1942, apart from the ASRS organisation – which in that year alone saved one-third of some 3,000 air crews forced down in the sea – a multitude of rescue and life-support devices had been invented. Chief among these were the Thornaby Bag, Bircham Barrel and Lindholme Gear; three varying forms of emergency supply packs capable of being released over any ditched crew like a normal bomb store, and each named after the RAF station responsible for its creation and development. Under trial also was the air-borne lifeboat which was later put to excellent use.

An outstanding example of the utter determination to retrieve any ditched crew resulted from a simple mechanical failure. On 12 August 1942 a Leigh Light Wellington of No 172 Squadron, piloted by an Australian Flg Off A. W. R. Triggs, was on an anti-sub patrol over the Bay of Biscay when one engine suddenly failed, leaving Triggs to make a hasty forced landing in the dark, in angry seas. Seeing that the automatic dinghy release had failed to function, Triggs prised it open with his bare hands then inflated the dinghy while his crew stood on the semi-submerged wing. An experienced captain, Triggs had already exercised his crew diligently in ditching procedure and, when the engine failed, instructed his wireless operator to send off an SOS signal to base with a rough fix location. Now, in the small hours of the morning, the crew climbed into the dinghy and paddled away from the sinking aircraft, baling water out continuously for the next six hours.

Throughout the morning a total of 11 aircraft were spotted, obviously searching for the dinghy, but none found it. In the early

Above: VLR – Very Long Range. Liberator GR VI of No 220 Squadron, KG869, based in the Azores, on patrol on 18 April 1945. /*IWM*

afternoon, however, a Whitley of No 51 Squadron saw the dinghy and released a Thornaby Bag and a spare dinghy near the ditched crew. The supply bag was gathered in but the dinghy floated away – it was to play a significant part in the subsequent proceedings. Signalling the location of the crew to base, the Whitley then flew off; but soon after a Sunderland, escorted by three Beaufighters, appeared. It was 'B-Baker' of No 461 Squadron, RAAF, piloted by the unit commander, Wg Cdr N. A. R. Halliday. En route to the dinghy the Sunderland had clashed with a roving Focke Wulf Fw200 *Kondor*, but shook off the German and flew straight to the dinghy. Another Whitley in the area, which spotted the dinghy and signalled down (by Aldis Lamp) 'Sunderland coming', was not so fortunate; it was shot down into the sea on its flight home.

Halliday circled the dinghy, sizing up the conditions for landing. There was a heavy swell, whipped by a 25-knot wind, but after jettisoning all depth charges and some 500gal of petrol, Halliday made his attempt. Triggs in the dinghy watched in agony as the Sunderland touched, bounced wildly over the next three waves, then stalled viciously into the sea. Its starboard wing-tip tore away, the starboard outer engine roared into flames, the main hull step shattered, and the starboard wing dipped into the water, dragging the flying boat down at the nose. The whole episode lasted less than a minute, yet the Sunderland crew just managed to release a dinghy before the crash. Unseen by Triggs, the flying boat crew – six men – managed to evacuate the sinking Sunderland and clamber

into the only dinghy, but this promptly burst. Flg Off J. H. F. Watson, the navigator, remembered seeing a derelict dinghy nearby (the spare dropped earlier by a Whitley) and could now see it, some 400yd away. Watson voluntarily swam to retrieve this dinghy but, having already suffered concussion in the aircraft crash, his efforts to reach the dinghy, though successful, weakened him so much that as soon as he climbed into the dinghy he collapsed into unconsciousness. When he regained his senses shortly after, there was no sign of his five comrades . . .

After a wet, cold, miserable night of fitful sleep, Triggs' crew faced their second day adrift. Throughout the day several aircraft were seen searching for them; then a Whitley of No 77 Squadron spotted them – only to be promptly shot down by several roving Luftwaffe fighters. At one point a French fishing boat passed within 400yd of the dinghy, but Triggs and his crew remained silent, not wishing to become prisoners of war – such was their faith in eventual rescue. On the morning of the third day – 14 August – the crew had their first meal, comprising a biscuit, a malted milk tablet, a small piece of chocolate, a small mouthful of fresh water. During the afternoon a shark began to take undue interest in their dinghy but was driven off. Another night passed, with the crew getting progressively weak from continual seasickness, water sores, and freezing cold; but on the 15th they tried to improvise a sail, and that evening drank a tin of tomato juice 'celebrating' the Friday night party usually held in their Mess back in England.

113

Throughout Saturday, 16 August, weather conditions deteriorated, with rain showers and clinging damp mist obliterating the sky, while the sea surface broke up in heavy surging waves which constantly threatened to overturn the tiny dinghy. That night torrential rain added to the crew's misery until daybreak on Sunday, 17 August. That morning the bad weather left them, leaving clear bright skies, and their morale was uplifted. Then at midday a Beaufighter from No 235 Squadron found them and the sole survivor of Halliday's Sunderland crew, Watson, nearby. Guided by the Beaufighter, Triggs' crew paddled for five hours to close the 1,000yd between them and Watson. They then managed to get Watson aboard their own dinghy. While they did this a Hudson of No 279 Squadron appeared over them and dropped Lindholme Gear.

At dawn next day three Hudsons and two Beaufighters arrived on the scene and mounted guard above them while guiding HM Launch Q180 to the spot. In the distance could be seen three Arado 196 floatplanes, while earlier Triggs had seen four Fw190s patrolling the area. Finally Q180 hove alongside and got the crew aboard, then began the journey northwards, escorted by three other naval launches. The tiny convoy was immediately attacked by a pair of Fw190s but these were chased away by the hovering Beaufighters. Late that evening Q180 finally reached Newlyn harbour and put the survivors ashore, where they were immediately rushed to hospital.

This epic of air-sea rescue had involved a total of 57 RAF aircraft – apart from at least 20 Luftwaffe aircraft in opposition – while the cost had been two aircraft and 17 air crew members killed or missing. It illustrated vividly to all Coastal crews that they could always depend on such total determination by their fellow crews and all rescue facilities if they were ever placed in any similar situation – a bond of faith which sustained many ditched air crews throughout the war.

Below: **Consolidated PBY-5A Catalina of No 63 PB Squadron, USN; the first American navy-air unit to operate from Britain when it was based at Pembroke Dock (initially) in July 1943.** */Author's Collection*

The Sea Shall Not Have Them

Although the RAF had employed maritime vessels from its earliest years, mainly in conjunction with its flying boat units, an air-sea rescue organisation per se did not exist at the commencement of war in September 1939. Indeed, the Marine Branch, RAF was not officially formed until 1948. At its birth on 1 April 1918 the new Royal Air Force inherited from its RNAS and RFC predecessors a grand total of 238 motor boats of widely varying shapes, sizes, and purposes; mainly for use in attending flying boats and other forms of seaplane. During the following 20 years progressive design of such vessels for specific air-sea duties was relatively slow and limited, but the need for a high speed, quick-starting, seaworthy, shallow draught vessel for (among other duties) sea rescue of crashed or marooned air crews had become recognised. By the outbreak of World War II just nine High Speed Launches (HSLs) were established at home and overseas' stations, and these few HSLs may be regarded as the true nucleus of the future ASR Service of the RAF.

By 1945 the ASR Service had expanded to include some 300 sea-going craft, backed by double that number of other vital marine craft for coastal waters' roles, with an overall strength of some 4,000 RAF 'sailors' manning the craft. During the years 1939-45 the ASR Service was directly responsible for retrieving approximately 14,000 men from the sea, including more than 500 enemy airmen. Yet during the first year of war all such rescues depended to a high degree on a loosely-knit peacetime cooperation between the Royal Navy, Royal Naval Lifeboat Institution, Coastguard Services and the GPO. By April 1940 an attempt to co-ordinate all such sea rescue procedures was introduced by Fighter Command's Movements Liaison Section; but in July 1940 the commander of 11 Group, Fighter Command, AVM Keith Park joined forces with Vice-Admiral Sir Bertram Ramsey (Vice-Adm RN, Dover) in organising a local rescue service with RAF HSL's, naval light craft and a handful of Westland Lysander aircraft 'borrowed' from Army Co-operation Command. On 22 August the Deputy CAS, AVM Arthur Harris, called a high-level meeting at Air Ministry to initiate a draft organisation for all air-sea rescue craft. The result was that the RAF remained responsible for the air search, followed by naval rescue, and overall operational control was in the capable hands of the Royal Navy. Within the RAF the ASR responsibility was officially transferred from Fighter Command to the aegis of Coastal Command with effect from 1 February 1941; and in the following August executive control over all air-sea rescue operations was vested in the AOC-in-C, RAF Coastal Command. The existing Directorate of ASR at Air Ministry was also merged into the wider Directorate-General of Aircraft Safety.

In September 1941 the existing Lysander and Walrus aircraft already employed on ASR duties were officially formed into RAF squadrons (initially Nos 275-278), which remained in Fighter Command, based at suitable coastal locations. In the interim an astonishingly varied selection of survival and rescue aids had been developed for individual use by ditched air crews; while air-dropped items for sustenance included various forms of survival kits originated by different RAF Coastal stations, and by 1943 came the introduction of the airborne lifeboat. The value of such devices may be scaled against the fact that throughout 1942 alone of a total of approximately 3,000 airmen known to have ditched, 1,016 were rescued by the ASR and its allied services. In 1943 this total rose to 1,684. By the start of 1944 the ASR Service possessed 32 marine craft units equipped with HSLs, based around Britain's coastline, apart from the immediate back-up services of ASR squadrons and a variety of RN amphibious aircraft at constant readiness to respond to every call, day or night, and in almost any conditions of weather.

By the summer of 1943, with both the Atlantic battle and the combined RAF/USAAF bombing campaign against Germany reaching peaks of intensity, the sheer 'value' of the air-sea rescue organisation was incalculable. Hundreds of air crews, forced to take a swim after their crippled aircraft had been ditched successfully, were gathered in safely and, after a few weeks or even days, were fit to return to their section of the air

Above: **Hudson III, V9158, which was used to test the airborne lifeboat Mk 1, designed by the celebrated yachtsman Uffa Fox.** */MOD (Air)*

war. The psychological effect on all crews of knowing that if they were forced down in inhospitable waters immediate help was already on its way was a tremendous boost to morale and confidence. Facing death on every sortie was already an enormous mental strain; the realisation that every effort would be made to retrieve them from the additional hazards of a sea ditching relieved the crews' minds of such extra doubts and worrying.

In perhaps one of the greatest concentrated periods of ASR success, a total of 101 British and American airmen were rescued from the North Sea alone in a span of just 50 hours during late July 1943. On 25 July, following Bomber Command's massive attack on Hamburg, USAAF B-17 Fortresses raided targets in northern Germany and 19 B-17s were reported missing. The first SOS from one of these Fortresses was received by a Coastal Command Group flying control officer in the late afternoon. As the attacks continued – RAF Bomber Command assaulted Essen on 25/26 July and the USAAF attacked Hamburg again, by day, on 26 July – reports of ditched aircraft came in on an escalating scale, and the ASR services began to intensify. HSLs, Walrus aircraft, lifeboats,

trawlers, fishing smacks and RN vessels all cooperated in the urgent search for the survivors; while airborne lifeboats carried by ASR aircraft were twice dropped in one day and once subsequently for located dinghies some 200 miles apart.

During the 50-hour period, which ended at 1930 on 27 July, more than 200 aircraft from Bomber, Fighter, Coastal Commands of the RAF, and bombers of the USAAF, took part in the day and night search operations, in addition to providing an air umbrella for every dinghy located until surface vessels hove alongside the helpless crews on the water. Most of these were over 100 miles from the English coast, almost halfway across the North Sea. Though a few air crews were spotted by the ever-alert Royal Observer Corps and therefore rescued relatively close to shore, one crew of nine Americans was saved some 200 miles out – only 60 miles from the Dutch coast – by the dropping of an airborne lifeboat.

On the Sunday evening when the first of a mounting flood of ditched aircraft reports began flowing in to the Coastal Command Group flying control centre, the senior FC officer remarked:

Above: **High Speed Launch (HSL) 2734, 1944.**/*MOD (Air)*

Left: **Rescue Launch 1250 in 1945.**/*Author's Collection*

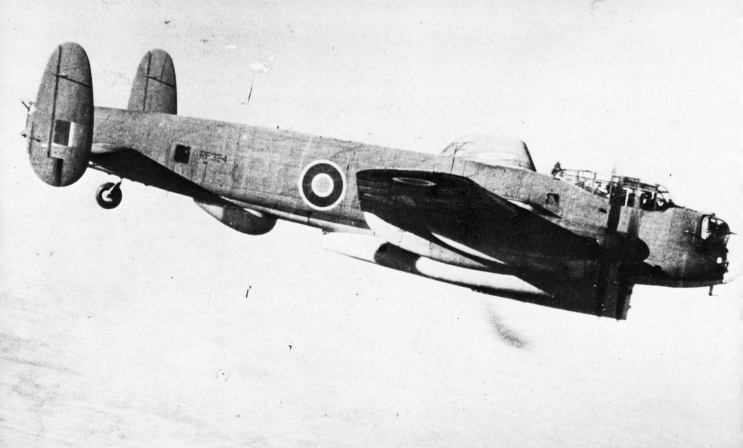

Five successive views of an airborne lifeboat drop from Lancaster III, RF324, 'K' of No 279 Squadron, based at Thornaby in 1945. Note H2S under fuselage. Final view shows rescued crew aboard the lifeboat, with full power on./*Author's Collection*

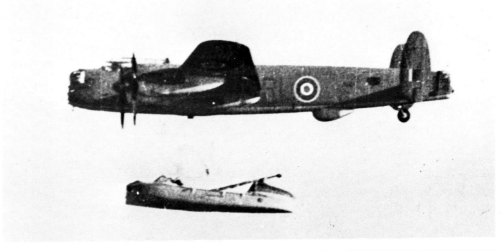

'I've never known anything like it before. On the second afternoon alone we had as many as 50 reports about dinghies which had been sighted. Positions poured in – from the ditching aircraft, from aircraft flying over the North Sea, from radio stations, launches, RAF stations and commands.'

Each message was recorded by a WAAF and, after careful analysis, fixes were obtained and the duty WAAF at flying control helped to plot exact locations. Then the rescue machinery swung into action. At one period more than 70 search aircraft were in the air at the same time – Fortresses, Halifaxes, Stirlings, Beaufighters – and immediate reliefs for these were required as each reached the limits of its endurance.

One airborne lifeboat was dropped shortly after noon on 26 July, when Wg Cdr B. G. Corry, DFC, spotted an American Fortress which had just ditched about two miles away. 'The crew had clambered out on to the wings and were getting into two dinghies. Three men were in one dinghy and another was in the water. When the dinghies started drifting apart I decided to drop the lifeboat. Down it went, landing like a leaf on the water, between one of the dinghies and the sinking aircraft. The air crew quickly boarded it and, as I left, it was chugging back to land, with another aircraft providing air cover. The survivors couldn't have been in the water for more than a few minutes.'

Later that same afternoon a report came in of a Fortress ditched 60 miles north of Borkum. An airborne lifeboat was immediately sent out, as it was known that the area was heavily mined and therefore dangerous for surface vessels to attempt a rescue. The pilot said later:
'We dropped the lifeboat without difficulty, and the American boys scrambled aboard it. There were nine of them and we stayed to give them air protection until darkness came.'

At dawn next morning more aircraft were sent to locate this lifeboat and escort it home. They soon found it and launches were despatched to meet it, while relief aircraft dropped extra supplies of fuel to the seaborne crew.

About noon on 27 July it was reported that a foreign trawler had stopped the lifeboat, taken the airmen aboard, and was heading towards enemy territory. An RAF Halifax was sent out, swept low over the trawler several times 'making threatening gestures', and finally persuaded the trawler to turn about and head for England. Its journey was closely escorted by RAF fighters.

Elsewhere two ASR Walrus aircraft rescued the entire 10-man crew of a USAAF Fortress. An Anson, with a Spitfire escort, sighted a

Above: Flt Lt G. F. L. Coates, commanding officer of the High Speed Launch Base, Dover in the early part of the war. Coates was awarded a Distinguished Service Cross (DSC) for his outstanding services – the first RAF officer of World War II to receive this naval honour./*Author's Collection*

Left: A scene epitomising the blend of airborne and sea-going assistance available for rescue services. Sunderlands of No 10 Squadron, RAAF, Catalinas, ASR Launches and RAF pinnaces – a true air-sea complex./*IWM*

Ventura bomber circling over 10 men in a dinghy, and pin-pointed the position to two Walruses of the same squadron, which immediately flew to the spot. These came down on the sea safely and took aboard all 10 Americans, but a heavy swell made take-off with the extra weight impossible. Unperturbed the Walrus pilots proceeded to taxi back towards England's east coast. For an hour both amphibians battled their way through heavy seas until they were met by a launch, which relieved them of the 10 men. One Walrus was then able to take off and return to base albeit in somewhat battered condition; but its companion still could not get airborne and had to continue taxying home; reaching port safely some eight hours later.

Another ASR squadron picked up two Canadian squadron leaders who had bailed out of burning Spitfires a few miles off the French coast. Spitfires which escorted a Walrus almost to the mouth of the Somme estuary fought off attempts by Luftwaffe fighters to hamper the Walrus, and shot down a Messerschmitt Bf109. The Walrus, with sublime impartiality, then calmly rescued both the Canadian and German pilots and flew back to base with its bonus. The second Canadian was rescued the next afternoon having spent the time in the sea supported solely by his Mae West life-preserver waistcoat.

Of the 101 crew members rescued during these hectic 50 hours, 59 (49 of these Americans) were picked up by HSLs of the RAF and RN; 20 by RNLI lifeboats from Sheringham and Cromer; 13 by Walrus aircraft; and nine by various trawlers. The Royal Observer Corps also sighted two crews a few miles off the Norfolk coast and signalled out the Cromer lifeboat, which rescued a 10-men American crew and a five-man RAF crew. Another ROC post saw a USAAF Fortress ditch not far from shore and signalled a nearby fishing vessel to the spot quickly. Yet another Fortress crew had been pulled out of the North Sea by a passing trawler.

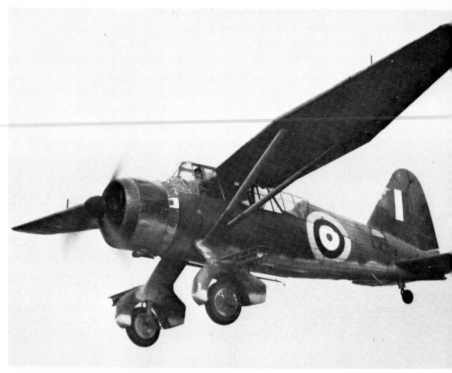

Above: The first true RAF ASR aircraft, the Westland Lysander was nevertheless mainly employed on such duties by Fighter Command from 1940. Only later did Coastal Command receive overall control of ASR administration et al. The Lysander's stub 'spat-wings' were utilised to carry and drop specially designed Type M dinghies, food containers etc. The Lysander pictured here, L4738, was a Mk I, and still retains its army cooperation message hook under the fuselage. /*Author's Collection*

Left: Pigeon-holes. WO McKinnon, RNZAF about to take his two pigeons aboard his Liberator, 26 February 1944./*IWM*

Above right: Warwick AS Mk I, HG214 of No 279 Squadron at Reykjavik, Iceland in July 1945. Fully armed in three gun turrets, the aircraft is loaded with an airborne lifeboat, and displays radar masts under wings./*K. Border*

Right: Vickers Warwick 'B-Baker' about to be loaded with an airborne lifeboat, Azores, 8 April 1945. Note Yaqi and other radar antennae under wings./*IWM*

Honour the Brave

The whole question of awards and decorations for bravery, courage, devotion to duty, or any other Service official 'qualification' tends to be a contentious subject in debate, particularly in Service circles. It can be argued that a Serviceman is simply carrying out his sworn duty in *every* circumstance – or as the layman might put it, 'That's what he's paid for'. Alternatively it might truthfully be stated that there is nevertheless a norm of duty; above which level of endurance, effort – or sacrifice – should be specially marked by individual recognition. The pros and cons of such a debate have no place here, yet no account of Coastal Command's story can fail to include even a few of the more outstanding men whose deeds, selflessness, uncommon courage and splendid determination to fulfil their given duties are now an integral part of RAF traditions and history.

The very nature of the Command's overall task offered little opportunity for individual deeds to receive any publicity comparable with the more glamorous exploits of the dashing fighter pilot, or the doughty accomplishments of the bomber crew member. The sheer grinding monotony and distinctly individual nature of the bulk of Coastal activities precluded wide acclaim by the layman public; paradoxically so when one considers the supremely vital part that Coastal Command actually played in the prosecution of the struggle against Nazidom. Nevertheless, if only in esoteric Service circles, a number of air crew became widely known by reputation or for some specific action. In detailing, however briefly, the more well-acclaimed individual's story here, it is emphasised that such men greatly exemplified the many hundreds of other unknown men of Coastal who patiently and steadfastly pursued their duties, without ever reaching the public eye or ear. The star-turns (in RAF slang) were simply the tiny peak of a dimly-seen iceberg of other crews who formed the vast majority which gained the final victory. Each man played his part, however anonymous, and – as with the legendary Battle of Britain pilots of Fighter Command – it was the combined effort of the unpublicised and publicised crews, both air and ground, which brought ultimate success.

Of the 32 airmen awarded a Victoria Cross for aerial operations during 1939-45, just four went to men of the maritime air struggle. One of these, though (pedantically speaking) not under the aegis of RAF Coastal Command at the time of the action which later brought him the supreme honour posthumously, received the VC for an action typifying to the ultimate degree the utter determination of all Coastal skippers in completing a given task. And, uniquely, his award resulted solely from evidence supplied by the very men he tried to kill. He was Lloyd Allan Trigg, VC, DFC, RNZAF. Born in North Auckland, New Zealand, Trigg was 27 years old when he initially enlisted in the RNZAF in June 1941; a married man, with two sons, who might well have sought deferment from active service had he so chosen. After the normal stages of pilot training in New Zealand and Canada, he was commissioned in January 1942, and a year later joined his first operational unit, No 200 Squadron, flying Lockheed Hudsons from Yundum airfield in West Africa.

With the nearby No 95 Squadron (Short Sunderlands) at Half Die Camp, Bathurst, the two units were tasked with aerial cover for all mercantile shipping passing through West African coastal waters. These units were joined by No 204 Squadron (Sunderlands) on August 1943. Trigg, a tall, quiet man, was summed up by one of his fellow pilots as 'He seldom spoke, but had a fantastic determination. He hated the Germans, and his sole interest was in getting the war won so that he could return to his family.' That determination was manifested during Trigg's first four months of operations, during which time he flew a variety of convoy protection and anti-submarine sorties, and on at least two occasions sighted and attacked U-boats. His constant keenness to fly on operations and dedication to his tasks led to the award – rare in that operational theatre – of a DFC, which was gazetted 16 June 1943 (though official notification of this did not reach No 200 Squadron until after Trigg's death).

viating run at the U-boat despite the steady hail of cannon shells facing him. Roaring in from the submarine's port quarter, the Liberator boomed over U-468 at only 50ft, releasing a stick of six depth charges; two of which erupted within six feet of the vessel's hull. Then, ablaze and still diving, the bomber crashed into the sea some 300yd beyond the U-boat, and the wing fuel tanks exploded on impact.

Unknown to Trigg's crew, their victim was shattered. Some 20 German sailors managed to evacuate the doomed hull, but several were immediately killed by predatory sharks and barracuda, leaving ultimately just Schamong, his 1st lieutenant, and five others. These survivors found a rubber dinghy from the Liberator nearby, and scrambled into it. Next day Sunderland 'H' of No 204 Squadron located the dinghy and directed HMS *Clarkia* to the spot. Once back in England Schamong and his men were interrogated, and during this investigation the Germans expressed outspoken admiration for the courage of the Liberator's crew and their performance. From such first-hand evidence a recommendation was forwarded that Lloyd Trigg should be awarded a posthumous VC; and this was approved and gazetted on 2 November 1943.

The third VC to be awarded to a Coastal skipper went to a Canadian, David Ernest

Left: **Flg Off Lloyd Allan Trigg, VC, DFC, RNZAF, of No 200 Squadron, RAF.** */Mrs N. Trigg*

Below: **Lloyd A. Trigg, VC, DFC, while under training as a pilot in Canada, 1942.** */Mrs N. Trigg*

In May Trigg's crew, along with two other crews, were sent to Nassau, in the Bahamas, there to convert to Liberators which were earmarked to replace the squadron's Hudsons. Completing the OTU training, Trigg next went to Dorval, Quebec where he took possession of a new Liberator, and then flew it, via Britain, to No 200 Squadron, arriving in July. Finally, on the morning of 11 August 1943, Lloyd Trigg set out on his first Liberator sortie, flying Liberator BZ832 'D'. His brief was routine – an anti-submarine and shipping cover patrol. A little more than two hours later, when some 240 miles southwest of Dakar, Trigg spotted a surfaced U-boat and immediately began an attack run. His target was the U-468, commanded by Oberleutnant zur See Clemens Schamong (his first command), on only its third war patrol. Having failed to rendezvous with his refuelling submarine U-462, which unknown to him had been sunk, Schamong was on his return trip to base at La Pallice when Trigg's Liberator appeared over the horizon.

As the Liberator bore down towards him Schamong order his flak crew to engage, and the Germans' twin 20mm cannons opened fire at long range. Their aim was accurate and they could see the aircraft was on fire in its centre section. The damage to the Liberator did not deter Trigg, who continued an unde-

Right: Lloyd A. Trigg, VC, DFC (second from left) with his No 200 Squadron Hudson crew, early 1943, West Africa. From left: Bennett, Marinovitch and Reynolds. All three died with Trigg on the latter's ultimate sortie./*Mrs N. Trigg*

Below: Flt Lt David Ernest Hornell, VC, RCAF, No 162 Squadron, RCAF.
/*Public Archives of Canada*

Hornell, a Flight Lieutenant in the RCAF, who was incidentally the oldest-ever air VC. Born in Mimico, Ontario in January 1910, Hornell volunteered for RCAF service three weeks before his 31st birthday – an age limit which would have automatically deferred him from compulsory enlistment. By 1942 he was serving with 120 Squadron RCAF in Canada, and in October 1943 was posted for active service with No 162 Squadron RCAF, to fly Consolidated Canso amphibians. At the close of the year 162 was sent to a new base, Reykjavik, Iceland as part of the far northern air cover for trans-Atlantic shipping convoys; and flew the unit's first sorties on 25 January 1944.

In June of that year Hornell was part of a squadron detachment based at Wick, and on 24 June, piloting Canso 9754 'P' he left Wick for a normal operational patrol northwards. Nearly 10 hours later, at 1900, Hornell was already starting his return flight to Wick after a completely uneventful sortie, when a submarine was seen some five miles off the port side, fully surfaced. The Canso crew quickly took up action stations while Hornell turned his aircraft onto an attack heading. At four miles range the submarine, U-1225, uncovered its flak guns and commenced firing. Some of the first shells sliced away the Canso's radio aerials, and during the following two minutes the Canso accumulated frightening damage. Chunks of the starboard wing were torn away, the fuselage was riddled with some shells exploding inside; while one particularly accurate burst shattered the starboard engine which burst into flames, burning the adjacent wing section from front to trailing edge. Bounced and battered by the

non-stop hail of flak, the Canso still bore in, with Hornell needing all his considerable skill to keep it flying on track with one engine feathered. At 1,200yd the amphibian's gunners opened fire, splashing bullets around the U-boat's conning tower.

As it reached 800yd range the flak ceased suddenly as the submarine swung itself broadside on, and Hornell flew across it releasing a perfect depth charge straddle. U-1225 took the full brunt of the consequent explosions, its bows being lifted clean out of the sea before falling back into the boiling foam and spray surrounding it. Once the depth charges had gone, Hornell climbed as

hard as possible; only to see the flaming starboard engine drop completely out of its bearings, spilling burning fuel around it. Inside the fuselage smoke was everywhere. Reaching an altitude of perhaps 250ft, Hornell already knew he had no alternative but to ditch his crippled machine. Edging into the wind he set the Canso down delicately and, after two horrendous bounces off the iron-like waves, the flying boat settled; its whole starboard wing and fuselage side aflame.

The crippled Canso took only 10min to slip finally into the deep ocean, but in the interim Hornell and his seven-men crew scrambled out and launched two rubber

127

dinghies, pulling well away from the wreckage in case of a fuel explosion. Only minutes later one dinghy blew up, forcing all eight men to depend on the sole remaining life support, a dinghy designed to accommodate four men. Seven managed to crowd into the dinghy, leaving just one man, Sgt D. S. Scott, a flight engineer, hanging onto the side.

As darkness closed in 50-knot winds whipped the sea surface into 40-foot swells, tossing the tiny dinghy about like a cork. Just before midnight a No 333 Squadron Catalina returning from its patrol happened to fly over and by sheer coincidence saw the distress signal fired by one of the ditched crew. After dropping flame floats and sea markers around the dinghy, the pilot radioed base for rescue services, then began circling Hornell's crew. He remained circling for 14hr, replenishing the markers at intervals, but during that time the second flight engineer of the marooned Canso crew, Sgt F. St Laurent, died from exposure and his body was committed to the sea.

Several times the dinghy was capsized by huge roller waves, but all the crew managed to get back into the dinghy afterwards. The constant icy soakings debilitated each man quickly, and David Hornell, though by then terribly weak and virtually blind, continually attempted to keep up his crew's spirits. After some 19hr afloat, Sgt Scott succumbed to the deadly cold, and the crew were forced to commit yet another friend's body to the sea. Finally, after 20½hr in the dinghy, a Sunderland brought an HSL to the spot and the six survivors were taken aboard and given immediate first aid treatment. David Hornell by then was unconscious in a coma from which he never recovered, despite the efforts by the HSL crew for the next three hours to revive him. To the very end Hornell had done his utmost to succour and support his crew, until even he was too far gone to do more.

They buried David Hornell in the grounds of Lerwick Hospital, and on 28 July 1944 the London Gazette announced the posthumous award of a Victoria Cross to him.

A third posthumous VC – though chronologically, the first such award to a Coastal Command pilot – went to Flg Off Kenneth Campbell of No 22 Squadron. Born in Saltcoats, Ayrshire in April 1917, Ken Campbell gained a degree in chemistry at Cambridge and, via the University Air Squadron, was commissioned in the RAFVR in August 1938. Mobilised for RAF service in September 1939, he eventually joined No 22 Squadron a year later. Equipped with Bristol Beaufort torpedo-bombers, 22 was then engaged in Rover patrols around the North Sea and coastal waters – seeking out enemy shipping for destruction. It took little time

for Campbell to settle into the operational scene, and in early 1941 he demonstrated his tenacity and determination by torpedoing a 3,000-ton vessel near Borkum on 13 March, forcing its crew to abandon the sinking ship. A few days later, flying Beaufort OA-M, he was out on a Rover when he ran into a brace of Messerschmitt Bf110s. Finally evading these he brought his Beaufort home, despite useless hydraulics, and crash-landed safely at base.

Only days later Campbell returned to the fray, putting a torpedo into the side of a 6,000-ton vessel off Ijmuiden. By early April No 22 Squadron was ordered south from its usual base at North Coates to St Eval in Cornwall. The reason for this detachment was the presence in Brest harbour of the German 32,000-ton battleships *Scharnhorst* and *Gneisenau*, which had only recently put into harbour there after a successful raiding sweep of the North Atlantic shipping. The potential menace of these two capital ships to Allied shipping instigated a week of intensive bombing sorties by Bomber Command, and one bomb dropped close to the *Gneisenau* failed to explode; causing the ship to be hastily moved out of its dry dock into the open harbour temporarily while bomb disposal squads attempted to salvage the unexploded missile. That same day, 5 April 1941, an RAF photo-reconnaissance Spitfire photographed Brest harbour, and revealed the vulnerable position of the battleship in Brest's inner harbour. An immediate attack by torpedo bombers was ordered for first light on 6 April, and No 22 Squadron was given the task.

At St Eval, only six Beauforts were available for a sortie at such short notice. The squadron commander accordingly decided to send three of these as ordinary bombers, ahead of the second trio which would carry torpedoes and make their attack as soon as they saw or heard the bombing threesome go in to the target. Captaining the three torpedo Beauforts were Flg Off Jimmy Hyde, DFC, Sgt Camp, and Flg Off Ken Campbell; for Campbell this was to be his 20th operational sortie. All three left St Eval between 0430 and 0500 on 6 April with orders to reach Brest and then wait for the bombers to carry out their part first. Unknown to the torpedo skippers two of the bombers failed to take off from the mud-bogged St Eval field; while the third, skippered by Sergeant Menary, lost its way and failed to reach Brest, and therefore dropped its bombs on a convoy near Ile de Batz and returned.

At dawn Hyde arrived over the outer ring of Brest in a fog of low clouds and dense mist, and – as per his briefing – circled, waiting for the signal (the bomber attack) which would send him in to the attack. Campbell, flying

Beaufort OA-X,N1016, had also arrived on time, and after waiting a while evidently assumed that he should attack before the daylight dispersed any low mists over the harbour. Hyde, circling still, spotted Campbell's Beaufort below him briefly, diving into the fog towards the objective and awaited results before making his own move. What followed was pieced together later from ground witnesses. Campbell made his attack at about 300ft across the outer harbour, then dropped to 50ft as the inner harbour's stone mole came into view. With less than 500yd between this mole and his target, Campbell roared between the masts of several protecting flak ships, then, as the mole came under him, released his torpedo and started to climb away, heading for the only cover available behind the hills surrounding Brest.

At that moment the whole defensive system opened up, and a withering wall of fire focused on the Beaufort. Nothing could survive in such a holocaust, and Campbell's aircraft was seen to crash straight into the harbour. When the Germans salvaged it, they found the body of Sgt James Philip Scott, a Canadian navigator, in the pilot's seat, which suggested that Ken Campbell had been killed or seriously wounded by the first flak shells. With Scott and Campbell were the other two members, Sgts William C. Mullins and Ralph W. Hillman. All four were buried at Brest in a grave of honour. In his dying moments Campbell's aim had been true; his torpedo struck the *Gneisenau* square on, forcing the Germans to rush it into dry dock immediately before it could sink. Eight months later the battleship was still high and dry, undergoing repairs; and only emerged from Brest in February 1942 when it made the now-famous 'Channel Dash' to German waters. Here it remained for the rest of the war – effectively out of commission.

When the reports of Campbell's last sortie filtered through from the French underground movement to England, Campbell was awarded a posthumous Victoria Cross on 13 March 1942; and in Sedbergh, where Ken Campbell had spent his early schooldays, they erected a memorial to the courageous Scot.

The fourth, and last, Coastal Command skipper to be honoured with the little bronze cross was another Scot, John Alexander Cruickshank. An ex-bank clerk, born in Aberdeen, Cruickshank originally enlisted in the Royal Artillery, but in early 1941 volunteered for transfer to the RAF for pilot training. Given his wings and commissioned in July 1942, he eventually joined his first operational unit, No 210 Squadron, in March 1943. For the following 15 months Cruickshank flew the unit's Consolidated

Left: **Flg Off Kenneth Campbell, VC, No 22 Squadron, RAF.**
|Author's Collection

Catalina flying boats over the North Atlantic on routine watch-and-ward escort protection and anti-submarine sorties; gradually building up a solid reputation as a skilful, patient, reliable flying boat captain. A modest, reserved man, Cruickshank was regarded by his Squadron as an utterly dependable pilot, who took his duties seriously.

In the early afternoon of 17 July 1944 John Cruickshank set out with a nine-man crew in Catalina JV928, DA-Y for yet another routine patrol from Sullom Voe; calculated to last some 14 hours. Just eight hours later, as the crew were thinking of the welcome return to base after a completely uneventful patrol, the radar indicated a contact on the surface, about five miles dead ahead. They were at that moment flying at 200ft, and Cruickshank immediately climbed into the cloud to cover his approach to the as-yet unidentified blip. Three miles on he sighted the objective – a submarine, fully surfaced and running at about 20kts. Ordering a recognition signal flare to be fired, in case it was an Allied submarine, Cruickshank got his answer – a heavy flak box barrage. It was a U-boat. Pulling the Catalina into a circling turn around the U-boat, he began an attack run, descending from 1,000 to 50ft as he closed the range. At 1,000yd range the Cat's nose gunner began splashing fire against the submarine's conning tower, and then the waist blister guns joined him in trying to obviate any flak opposition.

Roaring low across the target Cruickshank pressed his depth charges' release – and nothing happened. Banking tightly to port and climbing to 800ft, he completed his turning circle, shouted to his crew, 'Everybody ready?' – then, 'In we go again.' Below him the U-boat had stopped, giving the flak gunners a better chance to prepare for the next attack. Shells began slashing along the Catalina's flanks as it came in. Flight Sergeant John Garnett, the second pilot, described the events which then followed:

'We made a perfect run in at low level but when we were almost on top of the U-boat a shell burst in the aircraft. Our navigator was killed, and the skipper seriously wounded. I saw the stuff exploding inside; the front windscreen was shattered to smithereens and fire broke out inside. I received lumps of shrapnel in my head and hands; while Harbison (flight engineer) was wounded in both legs. The skipper just took no notice at all of the fire and continued straight on. He probably guessed our nav/bomb aimer was out because he timed and released the depth charges himself. It was a perfect straddle and the nose gunner saw them explode across the sub, followed by a violent explosion inside it.

'As we broke away I grabbed a fire extinguisher and helped put out the fire which had caught the inside bunks. The Cat had been hit badly. There was a big hole in the hull which we stuffed up with Mae Wests to make it fairly water-tight. There was a petrol leak in the engineer's position and the R/T was out. In addition there was a foot-long gash in the fuselage just on the water-line, which we stopped up with engine covers and more Mae Wests.'

Taking over control from Cruickshank, Garnett ordered one of the air gunners forward to tend to the captain's wounds. The gunner, Flt Sgt J. Appleton, continued the account:

'There was a jagged tear in his trousers and they were blood-stained. I managed to squeeze in beside him at the controls and started to cut away his trousers. Suddenly he went white and flopped over and fainted. Between us we lowered him down from his seat, carried him aft and put him on the only serviceable bunk. I dressed his leg wounds and only then discovered serious wounds in his chest – he had made no mention of these. We kept him warm with our Irvin jackets, but he recovered soon after and asked for a cigarette and something to drink. He was very thirsty, and had lost a lot of blood. Then he tried to get up and go forward, but we remonstrated with him and persuaded him to stay put. He asked continually if everything was all right, then asked how the navigator was. He must have guessed from the look on

Left: **Flt Lt John Alexander Cruickshank, VC, No 210 Squadron, RAF – the only Coastal Command VC to survive the war.** */Author's Collection*

Below: **Leigh Light Catalina IV, JX574 of No 210 Squadron over Sullom Voe, March 1944.**/*M. E. Street*

Right: **Catalina W8406, which saw service with Nos 202 and 209 Squadrons, RAF.**/*IWM*

Below right: **Flt Lt Gendehien, a Belgian with the RAF's No 254 Squadron, receiving a DFC award from AVM Hopps, Air Officer Commanding (AOC) 16 Group, Coastal Command, at North Coates on 27 March 1945.**/*Author's Collection*

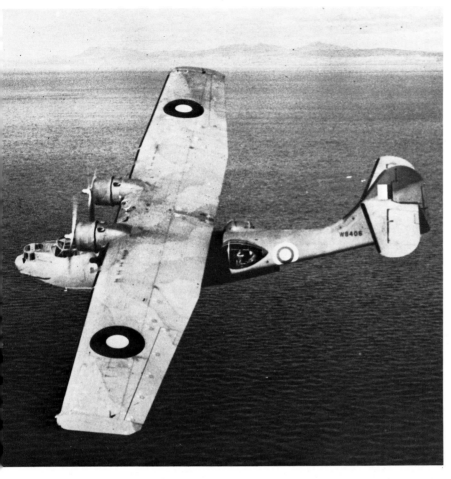

landed the Cat with the skipper giving him detailed instructions and helping physically once or twice despite the obvious agony of every movement. It was an excellent landing, but water started pouring in through all the hull holes, so the skipper ordered the Cat taxied on to the beach where it could easily be salvaged. The MO was waiting in a dinghy and came straight on board. The skipper looked just about finished when they took him out on a stretcher and frankly, we didn't think he could live.'

When the waiting medical officer climbed aboard and examined Cruickshank, who had finally collapsed from his supreme efforts, he had to give the pilot an immediate blood transfusion before daring to move him. On reception in hospital a thorough examination revealed that John Cruickshank had received a staggering total of 72 wounds, the most serious being to his chest and legs. By September 1944 both Cruickshank and his courageous second pilot Jack Garnett had recovered from their multiple wounds, and on 21 September both men attended an investiture at Holyrood House, where John Cruickshank was given his Victoria Cross, while Garnett received a Distinguished Flying Medal for his splendid part in the whole episode.

my face that he was dead. He looked sad, then said "Jack's the skipper", meaning Jack Garnett. Sgt S. I. Fidler, the 3rd pilot, making his first trip in a Catalina, kept check on the navigation.'

The Catalina crew saw nothing more of the submarine, but Cruickshank's attack had been accurate; behind them U-347, on only its second war patrol, had sunk. Setting course for base, Garnett knew it would take at least five hours to reach land, yet Cruickshank consistently refused morphia to ease his pain in case it bemused his brain. Lapsing into unconsciousness on several occasions, his first thought on regaining his senses was the state of his aircraft and crew. Appleton continued: 'When we reached base I went aft to see the skipper. He seemed slightly surprised when I told him we were over base. He said, "Help me up", and though we again tried to persuade him to stay where he was, this time he insisted and forced himself up, and I could see he was determined to have his own way. We carried him forward to the controls and put him in the second pilot's seat. Here he insisted that Jack (Garnett) should circle base for an hour until there was sufficient daylight to ensure a safe landing in our crippled condition. We circled and threw out the guns and other equipment to lighten ship. Then Garnett

From the Crews

Below: Two-some. Pair of
Hudsons of No 206 Squadron,
over the Brancaster area,
1940./*T. F. Kennan*

Only an actual participant's immediate reactions and descriptions can ever authentically reflect any specific event or particular period. Contemporary attitudes, personal standards in conduct or of morals, even upbringing are succinctly summed in on-the-spot personal accounts and reports. With a tremendous advantage of hindsight, the historian may well be able to parade a deeper, broader, even more accurate record of any past event – this knowledge having been simply culled from easily-available official documents and records in national archival sources. Yet no latter-day recorder can hope to convey completely the accurate feeling of the person who was there at the time in question. War, particularly aerial war, has become over-glamorised in a myriad of books, films, comic magazines, newspapers and other forms of the modern media; too often it is forgotten (or just ignored) that war has no glamour except to the perverted mind. War is about death, and about destruction on a vast, senseless scale; a reversion to the survival instincts of primeval man, where kill or be killed is the norm. The arrival of the aeroplane on the human scene merely offered yet another sophisticated means of inflicting death and agony on a so-termed enemy; whatever its other more peaceful applications.

The air crews, of all nations, who flew to war in 1939-45 found little to glamorise in their tasks. Too many saw their friends and relatives killed or horribly maimed to ever regard their job as anything but a distasteful yet necessary commitment. All were well aware that in carrying out their orders from higher authority they were laying their own lives on the line every time they took off on a sortie or patrol. It is a measure of such men's courage, loyalty to their country, and personal integrity, that they continued to fly, often daily or nightly, to face the unknown fate which was ever shadowing them. They were in the main young men, on the threshold of

Above left: **Beau boys. The Beaufighter crews of No 236 Squadron, commanded by Wg Cdr H. N. G. Wheeler, DSO, DFC, 1944.**
/Author's Collection

Left: **Mosquito 'A-Apple' of No 235 Squadron catches an enemy ship in the centre-stream of Dalsfjord, Norway on 23 March 1945.**
/ACM Sir C. Foxley-Norris

Above: **Terceira airfield, Azores in December 1943. After British-Portuguese negotiatoins, 'Force 131' landed in the Azores in September 1943 to set up an airfield at Terceira for (a) three Coastal GR squadrons, and (b) a Transport Command staging post. Maritime operations began in October with the arrival of two Fortress squadrons; later supplemented by Hudson and Leigh Light Wellington units. Designated as 247 Group, Coastal Command, the RAF presence in Azores finally ceased in October 1946.***/IWM*

manhood, with all the hopes – and fears – of buoyant, healthy youth; none were immortal, impervious to pain or utter fear. Yet they returned to the battle again and again – unfaltering. And those many thousands who failed to return left behind them an example of ultimate sacrifice which should never be forgotten.

The following selected extracts from personal accounts, experiences, and opinions authentically mirror the reactions of many of their fellow crews. Each is a microcosm of war, a scrap of genuine history. Most of the events described were 'just routine' to the individual speakers; one more experience in a flashing kaleidoscope of occasions which brought with them an intensity of physical excitement, mental peak, and on occasion utter terror, unknown to the individual involved before or since.

On 23 July 1941 the captain of a Hudson bade farewell to the convoy he had been 'escorting' for several hours, and was about to turn for home when a naval corvette below flashed a signal to him, 'Suspicious aircraft to starboard'. Knowing the tendency of all Royal Navy vessels to regard *any* aircraft as 'suspicious', the Hudson skipper at first thought the corvette had merely spotted the Hudson's due relief Wellington and, indeed, when first sighting the distant machine also believed it to be his relief on the convoy escort:

'I flew over to have a look at her anyway, and pulled down my front gun sight purely for practice. As we neared the aircraft, however, my Irish second pilot suddenly swore, then shouted, "It's a Kondor!" Automatically I increased speed while he ran aft to man one of the beam guns, the wireless operator manned the other side gun, and the mid-upper gunner swung his turret round. There, about 100ft above the sea and running in towards our convoy, was one of the large Focke Wulf Fw200s. We overhauled him fast and at 400yd I opened the proceedings with about five short bursts from my front guns, though I don't think I hit him. He returned the fire immediately from both top and bottom guns and I saw his tracers whip past the Hudson's nose in little streaks of light. He missed us and his pilot turned slightly to starboard and ran parallel to the convoy.

'I soon realised that we had the legs of him and soon caught up with him. He put up his nose, as if thinking to make a climb for cloud cover, but evidently changed his mind and decided that he was safer where he was, down close to the sea. As we drew closer my rear gunner opened up, firing forward, and I could see his tracers nipping across my wing. We drew closer and closer, and the Kondor began to look like the side of a house; at the end all I could see of it was part of the fuselage and two whacking great engines. My rear gunner was pumping bullets into him all the time. When we were only 40ft away I could see two of his engines beginning to glow. I throttled back so as not to over-shoot him, or crash into him, and for one brief moment my second pilot, Ernie, saw a white face appear at one of the side windows and then quickly disappear.

'Just then the Kondor began a turn, its belly exposed to us, and my gunners opened up with everything. There was a wisp of smoke, a sudden belching of smoke, and then then flames shot out from underneath both port engines. He turned to starboard, while I made a tight port turn ready to come at him again. We came out of the turn, only to see the Kondor again flying steadily, apparently unhurt. For a moment I thought he had got away with it, but then realised that he was getting lower and lower, and a minute later he went into the sea. I yelled, "We've got him! He's in the drink! We've got him!" The upper gunner too was yelling down the intercomm great exultant Yorkshire oaths.

Right: Crew of Fortress II, FA706, 'S-Sugar', which claimed the first U-boat kill from the Azores base. From left to right: Flt Sgt J. B. Fitzpatrick; Sgt F. D. Galloway; Plt Off J. B. Brodie; Flt Lt R. P. Drummond (captain); Flt Lt G. A. Grundy; Flg Off R. D. Thompson; Flt Sgt F. L. Fitzgibbon; Sgt L. S. G. Parker./*IWM*

Below: Puss in boots. Consolidated Catalina with amphibious undercarriage – known as a 'Canso' to the RCAF – in RAF initial delivery markings. This example, FP529, was designated Catalina IIIA by the RAF, and PBY-5A by the United States Navy. At least nine Coastal Command squadrons were equipped with Catalinas. /*Author's Collection*

'It was only then that we all realised just how hard and how silently we'd all been concentrating, and how full the Hudson was of cordite fumes. I also saw how short of petrol we were. We flew over the Kondor – its wingtips were just awash – and Ernie took photos. Four of the crew were in the water hanging on to a rubber dinghy which was just beginning to inflate, while a fifth man was scrambling along the fuselage. We learnt later that a Met man who had been aboard had been killed by a bullet through the heart, but the others were all right. Two corvettes were rushing to pick them up and the whole crew seemed to be crowded onto the deck of the leading one, waving and shouting at us. One man was waving a shirt. Our relief Wellington and Hudson were by now circling round too, and as we made off for home we could see the white puffs of steam as all the ships in the convoy sounded their sirens.'

Plt Off W. N. Armstrong was the skipper of a Leigh Light Wellington, operating from the Azores in 1943. Detailed for a night escort patrol over a convoy, he set out in brilliant moonlight and, several hours later spotted a U-boat ahead:
'There was a brilliant blue flash after my depth charges had gone down and I think one of them must have hit the sub. We stooged around for a while, then saw him again. It looked as if he was too damaged to dive, and my gunners opened up immediately, raking the sub from end to end. This time, however, he was ready for us and gave us everything he

Above: **Maritime maintenance. Engine fitters run expert eyes over a Catalina's port Pratt & Whitney Twin Wasp power plant, 12 June 1943. Note ingenious servicing platform provided.**/*IWM*

Right: **Tote that barge . . . Catalina crew ruefully surveying the kit to be loaded prior to any operational sortie. Apart from parachutes and navigation bags (left foreground), there are spare ammunition pans for the blister VGO guns; flame floats; smoke floats; sea markers; crockery; cutlery; food rations – virtually everything but the kitchen sink! Catalina AJ159, 'B-Baker' of No 202 Squadron in March 1942 at Gibraltar.**/*IWM*

Above: Briefing. Sqn Ldr Southall, DSO, DFC (centre) outlining a sortie for some of No 521 Squadron's Met-Fortress crews. No 521 Squadron – and other 'Met-Cal' units of Coastal Command were used on 'Rhombus' operations over the North Sea to the Norwegian coast; an unpublicised but vital, exacting role./*J. Rounce*

Top right: Fortress II, HB786 of No 521 Squadron, used on meteorological duties. Unusually for the period – 1944-45 – the aircraft serial is marked large under the wings. /*J. Rounce*

Bottom right: Though the Gloster Gladiator is most associated with its primary fighting role, as in the early war campaigns in France, Norway and the Middle East theatre, 'Glads' gave continuing splendid service in a wide variety of backwater roles until 1945. In particular they were used for meteorological calibration flights, almost daily, by most commands in the UK and overseas. In Coastal Command at least five units flew a handful of Gladiators on Met-Cal duties, including No 521 Squadron, and Nos 1403, 1560, 1561 and 1562 Flights. The Flight pictured, though unidentified positively, is believed to have been based at Langham, Norfolk in 1944-45 period. /*Author's Collection*

had. The flak was terrifying and it's a near-miracle we weren't hit then.

'I came round for my third attack run. The U-boat was clearly silhouetted in the moonlight, and I could see that the hull aft of the conning tower was under water, with the bows clear of the sea. My own gunners kept up so effective a barrage that the Jerry gunners only got off one shot before ducking for cover, but it was an unlucky shot for us. It hit our rear turret, smashing it and exploding right in front of the gunner, Flying Officer Heard. [Flg Off H. B. W. Heard, and his pilot Armstrong, were each awarded a DFC.] I didn't know about this at the time and only first learned what had happened when I asked over the intercomm what the rear gunner had seen of our attack. Back came the answer, "Sorry, but I'm afraid I must come out. I've been hit." He showed amazing courage and managed to lever himself out of the turret with his arms – he'd been hit badly in the legs. Despite his pain, he insisted on writing up his own report during the return journey – just in case he didn't make it, as he said – and was laughing and joking. At base, as soon as we landed, they rushed him to hospital where he underwent amputation, but he lived.'

Flg Off E. R. Baker was the skipper of Sunderland DA-H, P9624 of No 210 Squadron, based at Pembroke Dock, when he took off for a convoy protection sortie on 16 August 1940. To the south-east the legendary Battle of Britain was raging furiously over Kent and Sussex, but Baker and his crew were concerned mainly with the atrocious weather conditions

facing them during that early morning; driving rain with cloud base hardly higher than 400ft, in full contrast to the near-perfect summer's day on the other side of the British Isles. Six hours later the weather had hardly improved and Baker's crew decided to have lunch, if only to break the monotony. They had only just started eating, however, when the second pilot's voice sounded above the clatter of cutlery – 'Sub!!' Baker immediately sounded the warning Klaxon, and the crew jumped to their action stations. Baker reported later:

'I put my foot on everything. The U-boat was on the surface when we sighted it, and they must have sighted us at the same time for they started to do a crash dive. By the time the submarine was down I was diving low over the top of it to drop a depth charge. The result was terrific. The whole surface of the sea seemed to shudder for yards around and then suddenly blew up. In the middle of the boiling sea the submarine emerged with its decks awash, then sank rather like a brick. I did a steep turn and came over it again just as it was disappearing. The explosion seemed to have blown the submarine right out of the water – at least, there was so much of it out of the water that my rigger saw daylight under it. I turned and climbed, and as the submarine heaved on its side and sank I dropped my bombs right across it. Large air bubbles came rushing up – one was over 30ft across. Then great gobs of oil began to spread over the surface until a wide area was covered. I waited for about an hour until there was no more air or oil coming up, then I fetched a destroyer from the convoy and signalled what

had happened. After carrying out an Asdic sweep and reporting no contact, the destroyer signalled to me "Nice work. Hope you get your reward".'

Reaching base after nearly 13 hours of flying, Baker's crew made their report, and later Baker received a DFC. His victim, U-51, was in fact seriously damaged, but not sunk.

The U-608, a Type VIIC and one of the best submarine variants used by the German Kriegsmarine throughout the war, left Lorient on 7 August 1944, with sufficient provisions and supplies for an extended 14weeks' deep-sea patrol. By the early afternoon of 9 August the U-boat was shallow-submerged at a spot some 40 miles south of Belle Ile, off Ile de Noirmoutier, when she was spotted by a patrolling Liberator, 'C-Charlie' of No 53 Squadron from St Eval. At the bomber's controls was Wg Cdr Dick Gates, DFC, No 53's commander, flying his last operational sortie with the unit prior to promotion to a desk job at Command headquarters. His mid-upper gunner Plt Off A. S. Dantzic takes up the story:

'We were tootling along to have a look at an oil slick which covered an area of about a mile and was shimmering beautifully in the brilliant sunshine, when the beam gunner yelled over the intercomm that he's just seen a sub under the water. We all strained to look in the direction indicated and there it was – a long greenish cigar shape, with a darker green circle which was the conning tower. It appeared a lighter green than the sea with the sun shining on it, and the pointed nose was quite clear, though the stern seemed to be lower down.

'The skipper gave the orders for an attack and we swung down for a bombing run. The first time across the bomb doors failed to open, so the skipper circled to port and came in a second time, dropping our depth charges between the end of the oil slick and the U-boat from about 100ft altitude. The explosions were terrific and we seemed to be looking *up* at the huge fountain of water which erupted. Coming out of the run we turned to starboard and watched the results, the usual scum and oil. Homing some nearby Navy vessels towards the spot we stayed above the spot, watching in case the U-boat reappeared. The Navy arrived and picked up some planking and samples of the oil, but there being no other sign of the submarine we resumed our patrol.'

In the early hours of 10 August a No 224 Squadron Liberator, piloted by Flt Lt John Barling, got a radar contact in the same area, and on approaching in bright moonlight saw

Left: Equally, the ubiquitous Hawker Hurricane undertook side-show duties throughout the war. This Hurricane, coded 50-X, of No 521 Squadron, was photographed from a squadron Fortress while engaged on a 'Thum' sortie, ie a vertical ascent for met-calibration, over Langham. /*J. Rounce*

Below left: Eye in the sky. The value of photographic reconnaissance was only slowly learned by the RAF during World War II; but its mainly unpublicised role became of utmost importance eventually. Coastal Command played a major part in PRU administration and overall operational control; though PR remained virtually a private air force in spirit. Illustrated here is a Spitfire PR19, PS925 of the PRU. /*Author's Collection*

Right: Constant replenishment of Coastal Command crews with freshly trained personnel was a major factor of the Command's responsibility. Here three Catalinas from 131(C) OTU, Killadeas in Northern Ireland are flying over the operational base at Castle Archdale, June 1943. /*M. E. Street*

Left: Hallie crew. The Halifax bomber was yet another type used by Coastal Command when the need for longer-range and endurance became vital in the Atlantic battle. Nine squadrons flew Halifaxes with Coastal Command; one of these being No 518 Squadron, formed at Tiree in September 1943 for (mainly) met-calibration duties, such as 'Mercer' and 'Bismuth' sorties over the eastern Atlantic zones. This crew of Halifax RG414, Y3-V of No 518 Squadron was captained by Flt Lt. A. L. Milne; Tiree, May 1945. /*P. Rackcliff*

a U-boat sitting stationary in the centre of a huge pool of oil. He immediately started an attack run, only to be signalled by some Royal Navy frigates nearby that his target was a sinking U-boat, whose crew was already taking to dinghies. Continuing his patrol Barling later saw some 30 surviving U-boat crew men being taken aboard naval frigates. There was no sign then of the shattered U-608.

Terry White – inevitably, 'Chalky' to his friends – was a navigator in Mosquitos in mid-1944, flying strike sorties mainly along the French coast as part of the back-up to the recent Allied invasion of Normandy. Just 20 years old, and virtually exchanging a school desk for a seat in a Tiger Moth, then Oxford trainer, and now an operational Mosquito, Terry was no veteran. True he had some 20 trips under his belt but these had been mainly routine sorties with little excitement to report afterwards; 'thrilling to my young mind, but hardly dangerous' (sic). On this July afternoon however the trip looked as if it might be rather more exciting – a hunt for German shipping around the Brittany Peninsula, then a sweep southwards to the Biscay coastal waters. 'It was a marvellous sunny day with visibility right to the horizon – a day for flying in any sense of the word. There were 12 of us in reasonably loose formation strung out behind the leader, though not too loose that we couldn't close up quickly if any target worth clobbering appeared. We passed several fishing smacks and a few minesweepers but didn't waste ammunition on these, and continued along the coastline, keeping very low above the sea for most of the time. Each time we brushed close to shore we received splashes of flak – the whole coast seemed to

Above left: **Halifax P-Peter (LK966) of No 518 Squadron, usually piloted by Sqn Ldr Young, at Aldergrove. Note all-white finish.**/*J. O. Friend*

Left: **Halifax GRII, Series I Special, 'V-Victor' of No 502 Squadron AAF, over St Davids at 2,000ft, on 8 March 1944. Halifaxes of Coastal Command claimed a total of at least 13 U-boats sunk or damaged seriously.** /*via G. Jones*

Above: **Victory in Europe. Crews of No 36 Squadron at Benbecula on VE-Day (8 May 1945) being briefed for 'Blue Route' patrols. The wall map at back shows the line to which all German U-boats were instructed to proceed, and then surface and surrender to the first Allied aircraft or ship sighted.**/*G. Jones*

bristle with isolated flak guns – but no one seemed to have suffered any damage from these and we pressed on. We soon found ourselves near the mouth of the Gironde and ran straight into really heavy flak from some shore batteries.

'The sky around us seemed to fill with filthy black puffs of smoke – everywhere I looked they appeared, burst, and whipped past our Mossie, and my stomach began to feel distinctly uneasy. My pilot, a calm Devonshire chap who wouldn't say boo to a goose in the Mess but was hell-on-wheels when behind a control column, took all this without a word and continued to plunge through it all, keeping station with the chap slightly to port and ahead of us. Looking over his shoulder further to port, towards the next Mossie I was horrified to see that its starboard engine was streaming thin grey smoke; then saw it wing over sharply and dive. We were too low down for that sort of manoeuvre – he must have gone straight into the sea at full power. It happened so quickly I thought I'd dreamed it; then knew I hadn't . . .

'Then the Mosquito ahead of us bought it – one second he was there, the next he'd disappeared in a blast of orange-yellow flames and smoke, and I felt the thumps of bits of him hitting our wings and fuselage as my pilot fought to keep us steady. He only said, "Kee-ristmas!", then went quiet again. Once on track and steady again we checked as best we could for any serious damage to our own kite. The dials stopped spinning and seemed OK everywhere, though on my side I could see a chunk of wing scored from front to trailing edge out near the wingtip. Both engines continued at full steam, so we carried on. Ahead of us I saw a large vessel broadside on to us and my pilot eased the nose down and

gave him three short bursts as we passed over him – probably just to relieve his feelings at seeing his drinking buddy buy it earlier.

'Flying out of that hellish flak into clear sky again, we banked out to sea then started back up the coast, having still found little in the way of a worthwhile target. We passed over the sinking remains of one Mosquito but couldn't see any sign of the crew. Drumming on northwards close to the water we continued searching the sea for something, anything to hit. My stomach hadn't quite got over the sight and sounds of that encounter with the flak, and I realised with some surprise that I was feeling very angry. Probably just natural reaction at being shot at, but a definite feeling of pure bloody-mindedness. My pilot suddenly increased speed, and as I looked through the windscreen I could see three what-looked-like minesweepers up ahead of us. Evidently my skipper had decided to have a go at these. We kept low and, as the nearest ship grew large he let it have everything in one shattering burst. I could see the run-up splashes of shells track into the middle of the ship, then smother the mid-ships section in a crazy mushroom of smoke and tracer arcs. One of its companions evidently was armed because a double line of reddish tracer whipped by our cockpit from one side, while the windscreen in front of me suddenly went almost opaque as one bullet ricochetted across it slantwise. My pilot pulled back on the stick immediately and we shot upwards fast, jinking on the rudder at the same time to spoil the gunners' aim.

'Levelling out eventually we took stock again, but apart from the crazy-paving look of the front windscreen we seemed to have been untouched. My skipper spoke for only the second time, "Cheeky bastards! They need a lesson in manners" – having said which he turned back towards the offending ships and dived to sea level for a second go! My stomach turned over with a sickly thump as I saw long lines of tracer reaching towards us again, though their aim wasn't so good this time and the bullets missed by yards. This time my pilot aimed at the bridge structure and plastered it heavily in one long, smoking burst which probably near-melted the gun barrels. Kicking the rudder from side to side he jinked over the ship's masts and continued to keep low on the run-out; then gently climbed to 1,000ft and circled. "Christ", I though, "Not a third time – *Please*", but I kept silent. To my utter relief he'd evidently had enough – probably realised we had little if any ammo left by now – and set the nose homewards.

'We touched down at base smoothly, but the starboard tyre burst, slewing us off the concrete in a ground loop which skidded us across the grass on one wingtip, but without anything worse happening. Both of us evacuated the cockpit rapidly – petrol was stinking the place out and I've always been in utter fear of being burnt. We heard later from the ground crew Chiefy that the starboard tyre had been hit by flak or something. Four Mosquitos failed to come back from that sortie – eight good men gone forever – and what did we have to show for it? One crumpled Mosquito and a couple of minor ships thoroughly plastered but by no means sunk. It wasn't worth it. For myself, there was a tiny aftermath. About three hours after our landing, I was in my bunk getting changed into best blue for a noggin in the local pub later, when my hands started shaking quite uncontrollably. The spasm only lasted perhaps two minutes, then I felt normal again. If this was the legendary "Twitch", I can only say I flew 35 more ops before I came off Mosquitos for a desk job – and only then because I caught pneumonia (of all things . . .) and was grounded by the unit Doctor. By the time I was declared fit for flying again, the war was as good as over anyway.'

During the closing months of the European war Allied authorities became highly aware of a possibility of the Germans making some sort of last stand in Norwegian territory. Accordingly the impetus of the many anti-shipping strikes by Coastal Command wings was heightened in scouring the myriad of fiords and inlets which lace the Norwegian western seaboard. Such strikes meant a long slog to and fro across the never-welcome and too often hostile North Sea, followed by a decidedly 'dicey' form of flying in and out of the high-walled fiords. The usual tactic was to fly inland among the snow-covered mountain peaks, then make the final attack approach in a swift dive down the side of a steep cliff or mountainside; aiming at a target often anchored close to the base of another precipice which left only marginal space in which to manoeuvre at speeds approaching 300mph. Even when clear of the target the Beaufighter and, later, Mosquito pilots faced a long, tight and narrow fiord in their run-out to the sea. Squeezed in on either side by towering, menacing mountain faces, it needed just one second's loss of concentration to invite disaster.

Based at Langham, Banff and Dallachy, the Coastal Strike Wings took the war literally to the enemy throughout the bitter winter months of 1944-45, and kept up the pressure until the eventual German surrender. 'We shall not easily forget that last winter of the war,' wrote one pilot. 'Taking off from the ice-bound or snow-covered field we sometimes flew 400 miles across the North Sea to find the Norwegian coast shrouded in mist or low cloud. Flying among the islands and into the fiords in search of ships hiding there was rather hazardous since some of the passages were so narrow that there was little room in which to manoeuvre.'

The following brief extracts from the operations record book of No 489 Squadron, RNZAF give a slight insight into the nature of Norwegian strikes – and the formidable casualty rate:

'*Sula Fiord, 27 November* Convoy of two large merchant ships and four escorts attacked by Dallachy Wing. Results of torpedo attacks not observed but many hits with rocket projectiles seen on 3,500-ton ship and one escort was set on fire and left sinking. Three Beaufighters were damaged but all returned safely. Reports subsequently received show that the other large ship was the *Fidelitas* of 5,740 tons. She did, in fact, receive a torpedo hit and sank as a result.

'*Vilnes Fiord, 9 December* Twenty-three Beaufighters attacked a 2,000-ton cargo ship. Showers of debris were thrown into the air and the vessel was last seen heading for the shore under a heavy pall of smoke.

'*Forde Fiord, 9 February* Thirty Beaufighters sighted and attacked a Narvik-class destroyer. The fiord is narrow and flanked by steep hills; consequently it was impossible for all the aircraft to attack together. They also had to fly through an intense barrage put up by both ship's and land batteries. The destroyer and two auxiliaries were hit. Six of our aircraft were shot down by flak and a further three by enemy fighters.

'*Egersund Fiord, 28 March* Two cargo ships and an escort vessel were seriously damaged after an attack by 28 Beaufighters from Dallachy. Formidable anti-aircraft fire was experienced and four Beaufighters did not return from this strike.'

Gallery

Left: ACM Sir Frederick Bowhill, KCB, CMG, DSO, who commanded Coastal from August 1937 to June 1941. Born 1880, he served in the Royal Navy, then RNAS during 1913-18, and RAF thereafter./*Keystone Press*

Below: Top brass. Some of the men who directed Coastal Command's fortunes, 1941-43. From left to right: AVM G. B. A. Baker, CB, MC; Air Cdre A. H. Primrose, CBE, DFC; AVM J. M. Robb, CB, DSO, DFC, AFC; AVM A. Durston, AFC; Air Cdre S. P. Simpson, CBE, MC; ACM Sir Philip Joubert, KCB, CMG, DSO (AOC-in-C); AVM G. R. Bromet, CBE, DSO; Air Cdre I. T. Lloyd, CBE; Air Cdre H. G. Smart, CBE, DFC, AFC. The occasion here was a Group commanders' conference at HQ Coastal Command, Northwood, Middlesex./*British Official*

Above: **AM Sir John Slessor, CB, DSO, MC, commanded Coastal Command from February 1943 to January 1944.**/*MOD (Air)*

Above right: **MRAF Lord Douglas of Kirtleside, who as ACM Sir Sholto Douglas succeeded Sir John Slessor as AOC-in-C, Coastal Command in January 1944, and remained such until June 1945. Lord Douglas died on 31 October 1969.**/*IWM*

Right: **Sqn Ldr (later Grp Capt) W. Hedley Cliff, DSO, of No 42 (Beaufort) Squadron in 1940-41.**/*IWM*

Left: An outstanding 'character' of Coastal Command was Wg Cdr Lionel M. Cohen, DSO, MC, DFC (far right) who was the oldest-ever operational air gunner, being 69 years old when awarded his DFC in 1944. Officially a 'Liaison Officer' at Coastal Command HQ, Cohen flew a total of 69 ops. He died in August 1960 at the age of 86. Seen here with a No 206 Squadron Lockheed Hudson./*IWM*

Below left: Wg Cdr M. A. 'Mike' Ensor, DSO, DFC, AFC, born in New Zealand, who served with No 500 Squadron AAF in 1942, and sank U-259 on 15 November, and shared in the damaging of U-595 the day before. In 1945 he was commanding No 224 Squadron./*IWM*

Below: Sqn Ldr D. C. Pritchard, DFC./*IWM*

Above: Flt Lt J. R. Weeds, DFC of No 224 Squadron. /*British Official*

Above right: Wg Cdr (later AVM) H. N. G. Wheeler, CBE, DSO, DFC, who commanded No 236 Squadron (Beaufighters) at one period./*Fox Photos*

Right: Beau Yank. Lt F. E. Huntley, USAAF, who flew Beaufighters with No 404 Squadron, RCAF, in early 1944 from Tain, Scotland. /*Public Archives of Canada*

Above left: Wg Cdr (later
Grp Capt, CBE, DFC, BSc)
R. E. Burns, DFC, a prominent
Strike Wing pilot./*IWM*

Above: Flg Off Michael Frank
'Babe' Suckling, DFC, one
of the pioneer PRU pilots.
Suckling achieved instant
'fame' for his 'discovery' of
the German battleship
Bismarck on 22 May 1941,
which started the events
resulting in the capital
ship's later sinking. On
21 July, however, during a
PRU sortie over La Pallice,
Suckling was shot down and
killed by flak defences. This
portrait photograph was
taken only the day before
his death./*via A. Brookes*

Left: Another pioneer
photo-recce pilot was Sqn
Ldr Alistair Lennox Taylor,
DFC. Joining the RAF in
1936, Taylor flew Fairey
Battles in France, then
transferred to PR work,
flying Spitfires. He was the
first PRU pilot to complete
100 operational sorties, and
the first RAF officer to gain
three DFCs in World War
II. He was killed by flak
while flying a Mosquito on
4 December 1941 to Bergen
and Trondheim.
/*Ball, via A. Brookes*

Top left: Kiwi kings. From left to right: Sqn Ldr L. A. Robinson of Auckland, NZ; Grp Capt. A. E. Clouston, DFC, AFC; and Wg Cdr C. J. S. Dinsdale, DFC of Te Kuiti, NZ. At this time, Clouston was Station Commander at Langham, Norfolk, while Dinsdale was Commander of No 489 Squadron, RNZAF./*RNZAF*

Far left: Flt Lt L. H. Baveystock, DSO, DFC, DFM, of No 201 Squadron, who sank U-955 on 7 June 1944, and U-107 on 18 August 1944. It was as a Flt Sgt with No 50 Squadron, Bomber Command, that Baveystock won his DFM; being second pilot to Flg Off L. Manser in an Avro Manchester on the first 1,000-bomber raid on Cologne, on 30/31 May 1942 – the sortie which earned for Manser a posthumous Victoria Cross award./*IWM*

Left: Wg Cdr D. G. Sise, DSO, DFC, from Dunedin, New Zealand, who served with Nos 248 and 254 Squadrons./*IWM*

Above left: Free French. Wg Cdr Max Guedj, DSO, DFC, who served under the pseudonym 'Maurice'. Killed while leading Nos 235 and 248 Squadrons on a Mosquito strike against shipping in Narvik Fiord in January 1945./*IWM*

Above: Wg Cdr R. A. Atkinson, DSO, DFC, of Sydney, Australia./*IWM*

Left: Grp Capt Max Aitken, DSO, DFC, leader of the Banff Wing in the latter months of the war. /*IWM*

151

The Inheritors

Below: The Avro Shackleton GR1 was developed from its stablemate the Lincoln bomber, utilising the latter's wings, tail and undercarriage to 'marry' a new design of fuselage. Replacing Coastal Command's ageing Lancasters and Short Sunderlands, the 'Shack' first entered service in the RAF in March 1951, with No 120 Squadron at Kinloss. This MR1A, WG511 of No 120 Squadron was photographed at Aldergrove in 1955.
/Author's Collection

Left: Immediate progressive development of the Shackleton was exemplified by the MR2 series – longer fuselage, pointed tail, improved crew accommodation, and an ever-increasing load of radar and submarine-detection 'black boxes'. This quartet of No 228 Squadron includes WR956 (leading), WR959 (starboard), WR957 (port), and WR953 (rear). /*Author's Collection*

Below: The MR3 variants of the Shackleton were easily distinguishable by their tricycle undercarriages primarily, while other improvements included Viper 203 turbojets in rear of the outer engine nacelles (Phase 3 types). Dorsal cannons were deleted, though the twin 20mm nose remote-control cannons were retained, and wing-tip tanks were incorporated for even greater endurance. This MR3 was from No 201 Squadron, at Kinloss, Morayshire./*No 201 Squadron, RAF*

Right: The myriad of additional instrumentation internally fitted in the Shackleton is partially illustrated in this view, No 201 Squadron, Kinloss. /*MOD (Air)*

Right: Pristine MR2 Shackleton on public display at RAE Farnborough, demonstrating the carriage of an airborne lifeboat.
/via P. F. Wright

Below: The world's first four-fan jet, long range maritime patrol/reconnaissance aircraft was the Hawker Siddeley Nimrod – a direct development from the pioneering jet De Havilland Comet airliner. First flown in prototype form in May 1967, and the first production model on 28 June 1968; the Nimrod entered RAF service in October 1969 with 236 OTU at St Mawgan, Cornwall; then equipped No 201 Squadron at Kinloss. Five more squadrons (Nos 51, 42, 120, 203 and 206) were subsequently issued with the type. Capable of cruising a speed of nearly 500mph, the Nimrod has a range of some 6,000 miles. AEW (Airborne Early Warning) variants were developed; while the maritime 'Hunter' Nimrod carries the largest array of missile and submarine detection/destruction equipment ever lifted by an RAF aircraft.
/Hawker Siddeley Aviation

Appendices

1. Air Officers Commanding-in-Chief

10 Group, RAF
1 April 1918   Wg Cdr A. W. Bigsworth, CMG, DSO, AFC

AOCs, Coastal Area
September 1919   AVM A. V. Vyvyan, CB, DSO
September 1924   AVM F. R. Scarlett, CB, DSO
May 1928   AVM C. L. Lambe, CB, CMG, DSO
October 1931   AVM R. H. Clark-Hall, CMG, DSO
October 1934   AVM A. M. Longmore, CB, DSO

AOCs-in-C, Coastal Command
14 July 1936   AM Sir Arthur M. Longmore, KCB, DSO
1 September 1936   AM P. B. Joubert de la Ferte, CB, CMG, DSO
18 August 1937   AM Sir Frederick W. Bowhill, KCB, CMG, DSO
14 June 1941   ACM Sir Philip Joubert de la Ferte, KCB, CMG, DSO
5 February 1943   AM Sir John C. Slessor, CB, DSO, MC
20 January 1944   ACM Sir Sholto Douglas, KCB, MC, DFC
30 June 1945   AM Sir Leonard H. Slatter, KBE, CB, DSC, DFC
1 November 1948   AM Sir John W. Baker, KCB, MC, DFC *
1 January 1950   AM Sir Charles R. Steele, KCB, DFC
8 June 1951   AM Sir Alick C. Stevens, KBE, CB *
15 November 1953   AM Sir John N. Boothman, KBE, CB, DFC, AFC
5 April 1956   AM Sir Bryan V. Reynolds, KCB, CBE
1 June 1959   AM Sir Edward Chilton, KBE, CB
10 August 1962   AM Sir Anthony Selway, KCB, DFC
22 January 1965   AM Sir Paul Holder, KCB, DSO, DFC, MSc, PhD *
2 September 1968   AM Sir John H. Lapsley, KBE, CB, DFC, AFC *

*Received knighthood during tenure of office.

2. Statistics-Period 3 September 1939- 8 May 1945 inc.
(Figures amended to 31 May 1947 state)

Aircraft Lost *

1939	30
1940	324
1941	382
1942	447
1943	384
1944	356
1945	137

Total: 2,060

Breakdown by Type of Operation

Anti-submarine	741
Anti-shipping	876
Mine-laying	42
Fighter protections (ships)	78
Raids, land targets	129
PR	194

Total: 2,060

*Figures do not include aircraft lost 'outside' Coastal Command control, which amounted to a further 1,441 aircraft lost.

Casualties Personnel

	Aircrew	Groundcrew
Killed in action against enemy	5,863	159
Killed in accidents	2,317	535
Killed (other causes)	38	218
Wounded	986	49
Died of natural causes	23	224
Injured (other causes)	1,100	466
Total:	10,327	1,651

Personnel Strengths, Yearly
(N/A = Figure not available)

	RAF		WAAF		Dominions	
	Offs	ORs	Offs	ORs	Offs	ORs
1/1/40	1,108	10,585	Nil	Nil	N/A	N/A
1/1/41	2,480	30,334	160	1,690	N/A	N/A
1/1/42	3,500	51,091	338	5,885	329	815
1/1/43	4,593	52,793	384	9,877	898	2,796
1/1/44	6,657	56,527	430	13,149	1,680	3,863
1/1/45	6,682	63,842	486	13,311	1,874	3,292
1/7/45	7,029	54,261	495	12,492	2,181	2,697

Claims, U-Boats
(All figures minimums)

UBs sunk by aircraft alone	192
UBs sunk, shared with RN ships	19
UBs damaged	131

Note A total of 1,162 U-Boats were commissioned in the German Navy. Of these, a total of 727 were destroyed by enemy action. Of this total:
288 sunk at sea by aircraft alone
47 sunk at sea by aircraft + RN ships
80 destroyed by strategic air bombing raids
Of approximately 40,000 men who served in the German UB crews:
28,000 (approx) killed
5,000 (approx) prisoners of war

Mines Laid by Coastal Command-Controlled Aircraft
Period 1940-43 only: 1,224 mines (all types)

PRU Operation
106 (PR) Group
16,000 (approx) sorties
49,000hr (approx) flown
32 million photos taken (approx)

Air-Sea Rescue Operations
Period 1 February 1941-8 May 1945
(under Coastal Command aegis only)

Air crew rescued	5,721 (Allied)
	277 (Enemy)
Non-aircrew rescued	4,665
Total:	10,663

Bibliography

Coastal Command, HMSO, 1943.

Air Sea Rescue, HMSO, 1942.

Coastal Command Review, HMSO, 1942-44.

Battle of the Atlantic, HMSO, 1946.

The Battle of the Atlantic, D. Macintyre; Severn House, 1961.

The Battle of the Atlantic, J. Costello/T. Hughes; Collins, 1977.

Coastal Command at War, 'T. Dudley-Gordon'; Jarrolds, 1943.

Task for Coastal Command, H. Bolitho; Hutchinson, 1944.

Coastal Command leads the Invasion, M. Wilson/A. Robinson; Jarrolds, 1945.

Not Peace but a Sword, Wg Cdr R. P. M. Gibbs; Cassell, 1943.

RAF Yearbook 1938, L. Bridgman; Gale & Polden, 1939.

The Dangerous Skies, A. E. Clouston; Cassell, 1954.

From Sea to Sky, A. M. Longmore; Bles, 1946.

The Central Blue, Sir J. Slessor; Cassell, 1956.

Birds and Fishes, Sir P. Joubert; Hutchinson, 1960.

Years of Command, S. Douglas; Collins, 1966.

Penguin in the Eyrie, H. Bolitho; Hutchinson, 1955.

The Shipbusters, R. Barker; Chatto & Windus, 1957.

The Shiphunters, R. E. Gillman; J. Murray, 1976.

They shall not pass unseen, I. Southall; Angus & Robertson, 1956.

Twenty-One Squadrons, L. Hunt; Garnstone Press, 1972.

RCAF Squadrons & Aircraft, S. Kostenuk/J. Griffin; Canadian WM, 1977

In Full Flight, A. Spooner; Macdonald, 1965

Famous Maritime Squadrons of RAF, J. J. Halley; H. Lacey, 1972.

The Tiger Moth Story, A. Bramson/N. Birch; Air Review, 1964.

The Supermarine Walrus, G. W. R. Nichol; Foulis, 1966.

Avro Anson, A. Hall/E. Taylor; Almark, 1972.

Mosquito, C. M. Sharp/M. J. F. Bowyer; Faber, 1967.

Beaufort Special, B. Robertson; Ian Allan, 1977.

The Devil's Device, E. Gray; Seeley Service, 1975.

U-boat, D. Mason; Ballantine, 1968.

U-boats under the Swastika, J. P. M. Showell; Ian Allan, 1973.

The U-boat Hunters, A. Watts; Macdonald & Janes, 1976.

Aircraft v Submarine, A. W. Price; W. Kimber, 1973.

The Naval Air Service, (Vol 1), Navy Records Society, 1969.

RAAF over Europe, (2 Vols), J. Herington; AWM, 1963.

New Zealanders with the RAF, (3 Vols), War History Branch, NZ, 1959.

RCAF Overseas, (3 Vols), Oxford UP, 1946.

Destiny can wait, W. Heinemann, 1949.

Photo Reconnaissance, A. Brookes; Ian Allan, 1975.

Canada's Wings, 2 (*Liberator & Fortress*), C. Vincent; Canada's Wings, 1975.

Requiem

The Coastal Command Commemorative
Window, unveiled by ACM Sir Frederick
Bowhill in the Main Hall of (then) Coastal
Command Headquarters, Northwood on
13 July 1957. The layout of the window was
conceived and planned by AVM C. E.
Chilton, CB, CBE, then SASO at Coastal
Command HQ, and later AOC-in-C,
Coastal. Detailed design and construction
was by Aircraftman Norman R. Attwood,
a National Serviceman; cutting and glazing
by Messrs William Morris & Co,
Westminster; and the stonework by the
Croft Granite Company. This original
window was, regrettably, destroyed in a
fire at Northwood in 1969.
/HQ 18 Group, RAF, Northwood